Insider Threats Meet Access Control

Abdulaziz Almehmadi, PhD

ISBN-10: 1983529184
ISBN-13: 978-1983529184

DEDICATION

To my mother.

To my wife.

Abstract

Existing access control mechanisms are based on the concepts of identity enrollment and recognition, and assume that recognized identity is synonymous with ethical actions. However, statistics over the years show that the most severe security breaches have been the results of trusted, authorized, and identified users who turned into malicious insiders. Therefore, demand exists for designing prevention mechanisms. A non-identity-based authentication measure that is based on the intent of the access request might serve that demand.

In this book, we test the possibility of detecting intention of access using involuntary electroencephalogram (EEG) reactions to visual stimuli. This method takes advantage of the robustness of the Concealed Information Test to detect intentions. Next, we test the possibility of detecting motivation of access, as motivation level corresponds directly to the likelihood of intent execution level. Subsequently, we propose and design Intent-based Access Control (IBAC), a non-identity-based access control system that assesses the risk associated with the detected intentions and motivation levels. We then study the potential of IBAC in denying access to authorized individuals who have malicious plans to commit maleficent acts. Based on the access risk and the accepted threshold established by the asset owners, the system decides whether to grant or deny access requests.

We assessed the intent detection component of the IBAC system using experiments on 30 participants and achieved accuracy of 100% using Nearest Neighbor and SVM classifiers. Further, we assessed the motivation detection component of the IBAC system. Results show different levels of motivation between hesitation-based vs. motivation-based intentions. Finally, the potential of IBAC in preventing insider threats by calculating the risk of access using intentions and motivation levels as per the experiments shows access risk that is different between unmotivated and motivated groups. These results demonstrate the potential of IBAC in detecting and preventing malicious insiders.

Keywords

Non-Identity-Based Access Control, Intent-Based Access Control, Malicious Insider, Insider Threat, Intention Detection, Motivation Detection, Electroencephalogram, EEG, Event-Related Potential, EEP, P300, Concealed Information Test, CIT, BCI..

Table of Contents

ACKNOWLEDGMENTS

I would like to express my deepest and sincere gratitude to Dr. Khalil El-Khatib for his enlightening guidance, motivation, and vast knowledge and for the continuous support.

I would like to thank my family: my wife, my son, my daughter, my parents, my brother and sisters for supporting me spiritually throughout writing this book.

Abdulaziz Almehmadi

CHAPTER 1. Introduction

1.1 Overview

In our modern technology-reliant society, information security is an essential consideration in everyday life, with threats ranging from information disclosure that may incur public embarrassment, and loss of trust and reputation, to identity theft, to attacks that may result in the loss of innocent lives. As a result, security assurance measures have been improving over time to keep pace with the evolution of attack techniques. While various security mechanisms to protect the confidentiality, integrity, and availability (CIA) of digital information and to provide a safe and secure environment exist, *access control* is a main security mechanism that grants access to resources only to authorized entities.

Access control is the set of policies and mechanisms that determines whether to grant or deny access to protected resources to specific entities. Its purpose is to control who is permitted to access which resource, at what level, and during what time period. The purpose of any access control mechanism is to safeguard systems from unauthorized access to protected resources and to prevent security breaches.

Access control systems are composed of two components, namely authentication and authorization. Authentication is the process of verifying or determining a user's identity. Users whose identities have been determined or verified by the system are checked against permissions rules. The permission assignment for entities is the basis of the authorization mechanisms. The output of the authentication mechanisms is the input on which authorization techniques rely to determine the set of permissions to be assigned to each entity.

1.2   Problem Statement

"From those whom we trust, comes a great caution"

An Arabic proverb

Many methods for authentication currently exist. These can be divided into three main categories: "something you know," such as a password; "something you have," such as smart cards, tokens, and certificates; or "something you are," such as biometrics [1].

Methods from these categories can be used individually or in any combination. Failing to properly authenticate users might lead to imposters posing as legitimate users and accessing confidential information, causing numerous types of breaches and increasing risk levels. Authentication is the first layer of protection against unauthorized access, and without it, none of the other security mechanisms would work properly: an imposter who is mistaken for an authentic user can be a potential risk for any system. Confidentiality solutions, such as encryption to guarantee the secrecy of information, will not be effective in such a situation, since any imposter can access and decrypt protected data.

Although user authentication plays an important role in guaranteeing that only those who are authenticated and pre-authorized are granted access, statistics over the years have shown that a number of unpredicted and severe security breaches have been committed by authorized, trusted, and properly identified individuals [2, 3, 5, 6, 8, 9, 10, 15]. Current authentication methods incur high risks because recognized identity is not essentially an interpretation of good intentions; authorized individuals may abuse their privileges, voluntarily and sometimes involuntarily, because they are always trusted from the time they are enrolled into the system until that trust is revoked. Since all existing access control systems rely on identity authentication by design, they are not suitable for insider threat detection or prevention. Also, since a continuous evaluation of the level of trust in a user is not performed, the high risk of the insider threat remains the most common threat to an organization. In current access control systems, trust is established at the time of enrollment and is not changed unless an incident occurs that causes this trust to be re-evaluated. Privileges creep, which describes a gradual accumulation of access rights beyond those required to perform a job, is also a result of not regularly evaluating the level of trust in a user, which leads to a user having multiple access privileges that might be used in combination to harm their employing organization. The absence of regular evaluation of trust after enrollment and the lack of insider threat detection in access control systems leave organizations vulnerable to such threats.

It is a regular occurrence to hear about governments [3, 5], organizations, companies, and even universities facing insider threats [6]. Insider threats are a scary phenomenon that the current access control systems and methodologies do not have the ability to prevent. Organizations continue to invest money, time, and effort in security solutions, yet these solutions continue to fail to prevent insider threats [2]. Current solutions for insider threats are based on reactive-based approaches, meaning that organizations act when, an insider incident occurs, establish signatures characteristics of the incident, and then add an incident-specific policy or mechanism to prevent the incident from happening again to enhance its security solutions. An example is a statement made by General Tom Lawson, the Chief of Defense Staff of the Canadian Armed Forces, regarding an incident of a Canadian spy selling military secret information to Russia [5]. Following the incident, Lawson stated that "the military is reviewing its security procedures" [5]. This current way of thinking, employing signature-based solutions, might prevent the same incidents from happening again, yet in the insider threat case, a new and different insider incident may result in massive destruction to an organization from which it may not be able to recover. More importantly, as security specialists continuously analyze security incidents to develop countermeasures, attackers continuously update their attack tactics, as well.

Thus, there is an urgent need to design new access control models that are non-identity-based to prevent insider threats, or even to complement the existing models with non-identity-based features. Such non-identity-based access control models prevent insider threats where malicious authorized entities abuse their privileges, as these models overcome the weakness of identity-based access control models that relate an identity to a trust level.

The difference between identity-based and non-identity-based access control in this book depends on the authentication component. If the authentication component requires authenticating an identity, then it is considered identity-based; if it does not depend on authenticating an identity, then it is considered to be non-identity-based. Identity-based authentication methods disregard the reason of the access request at request time and may result in the exploitation of privilege accumulation. The assumption that a trusted entity will not become an internal threat introduces risk into the system. Such risk, if accepted by employees and organizations, might have devastating consequences.

Reactive security in the case of insider threat accompanies risk; thus, proactive approaches are always preferred. Being able to prevent an attack is far preferable to being attacked and then building signatures to detect the attack and prevent a similar incident in the future. This concept particularly applies to insider threats, since insider incidents are lower in number compared with outsider incidents, yet the impact of an insider incident is more damaging, given the knowledge that insiders have compared with outsiders. Instead of looking at what an attack is and what its target is to build reactive solutions, another approach is to consider the source of the attack, the insiders themselves. Jackson [2] recommended combining computer science with psychology in order to predict insider threats from the behavioral perspective. While we agree with Jackson's recommendation, this book examines the possibility of combining computer science specifically with cognitive psychology, which can provide cues into how an insider thinks, reasons, intends, plans, and acts. We target the insider threat from the access control perspective, since access control is the first layer of defense, and especially since it directly interacts with insiders.

1.3 Motivation

"Be cautious of your enemy once, but of your friend a thousand times"

An Arabic proverb

An enemy in this context is the outsider who is unknown to the system and is not authorized to access protected resources. Numerous solutions exist for such threats (e.g., firewalls, intrusion detection and prevention systems, and Identity-based Access Control), but a friend in this context is one who is trusted by the system and is not expected to be attacked by him or her. Another contributing factor to the problem is what is commonly referred to as the *trust trap*. This concept states that "trust increases over time, yielding a false sense of security because the trust leads to decreased vigilance toward the threat" [15]. The trust trap concept also highlights the severity of the risk that a trusted entity might inflict more damage compared with a non-trusted entity simply because detection and prevention techniques in access control are designed to stop outsiders, with no consideration of protection from those whom we trust, the ones whom we already allowed to pass through defense mechanisms, the insiders.

To protect against insider threats, a new dimension of access control is required in which access is granted based on the intention of the requester toward the requested resource. The need for this new dimension is intended to address the common risk, which is that all access control systems cannot protect from malicious insiders who have been previously authorized to access the requested resources.

There exist a number of approaches and systems to address the problem of users abusing their privileges, including Data Loss Prevention (DLP), in which data are inspected if they consist of sensitive information that must not leave the organization either via email or in a storage medium. Another approach is the segregation of duties, in which no task is to be completed by only one person. Awareness programs, in which employees are educated about the sensitivity of data and the consequences of abusing privileges, are also employed. Other common approaches include enforced guidelines, in which insider threat procedures and best practices are not only written but also applied, and log management, in which logs are monitored and investigated in case an insider threat incident is detected [8]. However, DLP is not effective if the administrator is the insider. The segregation of duties becomes ineffective if all parties agree to commit the crime. Regarding awareness programs and enforced guidelines, they are important, but not as standalone solutions. Finally, log management solutions are mostly used for auditing purposes, and not as a proactive measure for the insider threat. Examples of scenarios that traditional identity-based access control systems cannot protect from, and that have been reported and analyzed by the Computer Emergency Response Team (CERT) insider threat center [6], include:

1. An administrator changing all company passwords before job termination.

2. Insider deleting all backups.

3. Insider accessing user accounts of their former employer.

4. Insider testing logic bombs before implanting one.

5. Web developer adding pornographic images on company website.

6. Insider forwarding company calls to another company.

7. Insider leaking private information to media.

8. Government insider changing a living person's data to deceased.

9. Insider intentionally opening a malicious file to infect his company.

10. Edward Snowden, admitting that he leaked top-secret information about the National Security Agency's (NSA) surveillance, as he had a high level of clearance [3].

Many similar examples emphasize the need for intent-based access control, with possible deployment venues that include airports, military applications, border security, and even financial institutions, in order to detect and prevent terrorism, crimes, and insider threats, in general.

1.4 Proposal

To address the vulnerability of current access control systems with respect to insider threats, we investigate the possibility of using a novel intent-based authentication and authorization mechanism that denies access requests from a previously trusted entity who has become malicious or has the intention of abusing his or her privileges.

To study the possibility of using intention detection for access control, we investigate the possibility to detect intention of access and investigate the possibility to detect motivation of access. We then propose Intent-based Access Control (IBAC), an access control model that eliminates the assumption of identity to be equal to good intentions by examining the intention of each person, as opposed to existing identity-based authentication and authorization measures that provide access decisions based on associating access to identity. IBAC is a non-identity-based access control method, as it does not require knowing *who* is requesting access but instead *why* access is being requested. A user can claim an intention, but then needs to prove that claim. Because IBAC is a non-identity-based method, it addresses the insider threat, since an identity in the insider threat context can be misleading, and only non-identity-based measures show promise in mitigating such threats.

In this book, we select the measurements of physiological signals that are related to intention and motivation to calculate risk of access and to grant/deny access requests to protected resources. To the best of our knowledge, there has not been any study that has examined the intention of access to detect malicious, previously trusted, insiders or to combine intention of access with motivation of access in calculating the overall access risk. Our research work is the first to use brain signals as an intention detection mechanism for access control combined with motivation detection. Over the last decade and with the advancements in sensing and signal processing technologies, analyzing the user's physiological signals, including electroencephalogram (EEG), brain signals, has become possible. Our approach, the IBAC system, focuses on the use of EEG signals in order to detect intents of access as well as the access motivation level.

1.4.1   Hypotheses

To address the vulnerability of trusting insiders in current access control models that rely on identity, we developed a set of hypotheses that culminate in the following main hypothesis:

> **Main Hypothesis:** *Intent-based Access Control (IBAC) has the potential to detect and prevent malicious insiders by calculating access risk associated with the detected intent of access and the corresponding motivation level.*

To address the main hypothesis, we developed the following supporting hypotheses:

> *Hypothesis 1: Intention of access can be computed using human physiological signals generally, and brain signals specifically, by exploiting the self-knowledge existence of intentions.*

To address *Hypothesis 1*, we postulate that because people know their intentions of access, we can exploit that knowledge and detect it using their brain reactions to visual stimuli after stimulating their brains with the question "*What is your intention of access?*" Using the *event-related potential* (ERP) brain signals and specifically the P300 signal, a positive peak delayed by 300 milliseconds in the brain signal, we can detect with high accuracy useful knowledge about a user's intention.

Since knowledge about an intention to perform an action does not necessarily guarantee that the action will be executed, we propose the use of *motivation* to predict the likelihood of occurrence of the intended action. Motivation is the cause that pushes individuals to engage in certain actions. Calculating motivation provides the access control system a second dimension of calculating the risk of access. For example, a high-risk malicious intention with low motivation results in low risk, since the probability of the intention being executed is low. On the other hand, a medium-risk malicious intention with high motivation results in high risk, since its probability to occur is high.

Hypothesis 2: Motivation detection is possible using human physiological signals generally, and brain signals specifically.

To address *Hypothesis 2*, we theorize that the motivation level accompanying knowledge about an intention is detected using the P300 signal amplitude, and that this information can be used as a measure for the determination of the user to act on the detected intention. The methodology to test this idea involves designing two experiments: one involving hesitation, and the other involving high motivation. It is theorized that the P300 signal amplitude will be higher in the second experiment since it involves high motivation compared with the first experiment that involves hesitation.

1.5   Contributions

The research work presented in this book constitutes a contribution to the information technology security field generally, and to the sub-field of access control specifically, by:

1- Providing a design and development of a new method of:

   a)   Authentication that identifies and verifies the intentions of access.

   b)   Authorization that is based on the risk associated with the intentions of access and motivation levels.

2- Providing the design and development for detecting intention of access using EEG signals, as well as detecting motivation levels toward intentions of access.

3- Providing a method for answering *why* access is requested as opposed to current access control systems that ask *who* is requesting access.

4- Proposing and evaluating the idea of using and detecting motivation level toward requested resources as a probability measurement of intents being executed.

5- Designing an insider threat-focused access control system design called Intent-based Access Control, and testing its potential in detecting and preventing malicious insiders.

1.6   Organization of the Book

The rest of this book is organized as follows: Chapter 2 presents a literature review on the insider threat and the four theoretical considerations that inform this study, including the theory of identity and trust, intention detection, event-related potentials, and the concealed information test. Chapter 3 lays out the research objectives and methodology, including the IBAC design. Chapter 4 describes the experimental design to test the potential of IBAC. Chapter 5 presents the data analysis, reports the results and findings, and provides discussion about the proposed system including its acceptability, usability, privacy concerns, deployment, limitations, implications, and advantages. Chapter 6 suggests future work to strengthen the investigated approach by challenging the system from the sensor level to the application level. This chapter also addresses other areas of exploration that require investigation including considerations of accuracy, acceptability, usability, privacy, deployment, and limitations, as well as implications for the use of the IBAC method. Chapter 7 concludes the work by summarizing the main findings and suggesting future areas of exploration.

CHAPTER 2. Insider Threats and Access Control Literature Review

Four theoretical considerations inform this study of the insider threat: 1) the theory of organizational identity and trust [iv], 2) the theory of intention detection as a component of planned behavior theory [43], 3) the theory of event-related potentials (ERP) as a part of the brain-computer interface (BCI) field, and 4) the theory of the Concealed Information Test (CIT) [71].

The theory of identity and trust serves as the basis of the common vulnerability in existing access control models. It provides insights into why these forms of access control are incapable of detecting insider threats, as current access control systems mainly rely on identity determination. Planned behavior theory and, specifically, intention detection serve as the proposed solution for insider threats, where we verify the intention of access as opposed to verifying the claimed identity. BCI technology, specifically using ERP signals, serves as the adapted approach for intention detection. ERP signals provide information about the existence of knowledge about an intention that we can exploit to detect the intention of access request by applying CIT protocols. ERP signals also provide information about the motivation toward an intention. We use ERP signals to compute the likelihood of intention execution, which in turn influences the access risk level. Intention detection, event-related potentials, and CIT theories serve as the core theoretical components for the proposed Intent-based Access Control (IBAC). Figure 2-1 shows the main theories related to IBAC in this book.

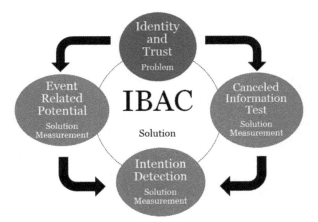

Figure 2-1. The Intent-based Access Control model and associated theories.

Before addressing each theory and explaining how it informs this study, we will provide information on insider threats and on the common practices employed to protect against insiders.

2.1   The Insider Threat

2.1.1   Overview

A wide variety of real-life scenarios exist in which an insider proved to be malicious, such as the trusted night-shift security guard who gained access to hospital computers and planted a malicious code that turns off the ventilation, heating and cooling systems, which could have resulted in the loss of lives [6]. The guard shared a video of his crime on YouTube, which was viewed and reported to police. Fortunately, the guard was caught before the code was executed.

Another example is the Royal Canadian Navy spy Jeffrey Delisle. The naval intelligence officer sold military information to the Russians and received $71,817 over 5 years starting in 2007, which resulted in "exceptionally grave harm to the country" as stated in [5]. A statement was made by General Tom Lawson, the Chief of Defense Staff of the Canadian Armed Forces, assuring that the Canadian "military is reviewing its security procedures" [5]. This review indicates an assessment of the insider threat mitigation plan, if it exists. This incident strongly confirms the need for an insider threat mitigation plan, as damage caused in this case is a matter of national security. At the present time, it remains unknown what information about the Canadian military Delisle sold to Russia [5].

A definition of *insider threat* as provided by the CERT Insider Threat Center states that *"A malicious insider threat is a current or former employee, contractor, or business partner who has or had authorized access to an organization's network, system, or data and intentionally exceeded or misused that access in a manner that negatively affected the confidentiality, integrity, or availability of the organization's information or information systems"* [6].

Because all insiders are trusted at the time they are committing their crimes, the level of access they have is usually higher than that of an external attacker; thus, the incidents caused by insiders are always devastating. Many such incidents are reported in [6], including an example of a chemist who planned to resign and work at a competitor organization, and who downloaded over 17,000 PDF files and 22,000 abstracts of trade secrets from the current organization's server, including intellectual property valued at $400 million. This incident and many other serve as illustrations of the level of damage an insider can inflict.

With the understanding of what insiders are, we continue in this section by addressing insider threat profiles, insider threat impact, and best practices with respect to prevention. We subsequently discuss the limitations of current solutions.

2.1.2   Insider Threat Profiles

Three types of insider threat profiles exist. These profiles were extracted based on similarity patterns among reported and documented incidents. Based on the analysis of more than 700 real insider threat cases, these profiles are: 1) IT Sabotage, 2) Theft of Intellectual Property, and 3) Fraud [6]. Details of each threat profile are provided in the next section.

2.1.2.1   IT Sabotage

IT sabotage is the crime profile involving a crime being committed using information technology (IT). This kind of crime is usually committed by technical users who have high-level access. System, network, and database administrators, as well as programmers, are examples of the typical IT sabotage-related crime offenders. IT sabotage is usually set up while the offender is still employed, but is executed after termination of the employment. This type of sabotage is done mostly for purposes of revenge [6].

An example of insider threat IT sabotage is presented in [6], in which a consultant and software developer in a company that manages client data and operations for another company had asked for a share in the ownership of the company for over a year. The company management rejected the request of the consultant and changed his status to part-time with a significant decrease in benefits. The next day after his demotion, the consultant logged into his account remotely and removed sensitive code in the production system, which resulted in the system going offline. Employees at the company contacted the consultant for support, but he refused to help. He told them about what he did, and requested a 20% share of the company, with the threat that more damage would follow if his demands were not met. As the management of the company refused to give in, the consultant changed all passwords in the company, resulting in disabling access to all employees. After this former employee confronted the management and informed them that he was behind the attacks, the company management reported the incidents to the police, who ordered the consultant to pay $10,000 in restitution, with additional sentences of 6 months of home detention and 2 years of probation.

2.1.2.2   Theft of Intellectual Property

Theft of intellectual property (IP) is a crime profile involving an insider using IT resources to steal intellectual property. It is usually committed by engineers, scientists, and sales representatives who are usually aware of the value of the IP. Theft of IP is mostly performed for personal gain, where the offender either uses the stolen IP in his or her own company, or sells it to competitors for a profit [6]. An example of insider threat theft of intellectual property includes a programmer who worked at a nuclear power plant in the United States. The programmer made a copy of the simulation software for the power plant containing schematics and engineering information for the plant, and transported the copy to his own country [6].

2.1.2.3   Fraud

Fraud is the crime profile in which an insider uses IT to maliciously change data for financial gain. As opposed to IT sabotage and theft of IP, fraud is committed by low-level employees such as customer service representatives, data entry workers, and help desk employees. This type of malicious activity might continue undetected for a long period of time [6]. An example of a fraud insider threat includes a police communication operator whose job was to provide drivers' license validity and vehicle registration information to law enforcement. After working for more than 2 years, the operator started to provide drivers' license information for money and to issue drivers' licenses to people who could not legally receive such a license. After being reported by an undercover officer, the operator was sent to jail for more than 3 years, as she had issued more than 190 fake drivers' licenses for financial gain [6].

2.1.3   Insider Threat Impact

Taking into consideration the crime profiles described above and the severity of impact they can cause, it is easy to imagine the level of damage that insiders can cause. Since insiders are trusted, authorized entities in their organization, who are assigned access privileges to valuable assets, and who know how to navigate through the company's systems, it is apparent that the impact of insider threats can be catastrophic. Malicious insiders pass electronic and physical security measures: They have legitimate and authorized access, yet they use the legitimate access to commit their crimes. The results of insider attacks can range from public embarrassment, and loss of trust and reputation, to millions of dollars in loss. Organizations might also experience operational impacts, discontinuation of product lines, or hostile activity, and terrorist attacks may also result, to list a few possibilities.

2.1.4   Insider Threats Prevention Best Practices

The detection and prevention of malicious insiders is not an easy task, as insiders are trusted with their role in an organization, yet use that role to commit their attacks. The difficulty of detection of insider threats lies in the fact that there is not any distinctive known general feature (gender, age, ethnicity, etc.) to indicate the hostile intent of an insider.

The CERT Insider Threat Center released the following set of best practices in order to prevent insider threats [6]:

1) Consider threats from insiders and business partners in enterprise-wide risk assessment processes. The difficulty of malicious insiders and business partners detection lies in the fact that they are trusted to carry out their roles within the organization. Using their roles and privileges, and knowledge of the vulnerabilities within the organization, insiders become able to attack the valuable assets of the organization. The best practice suggests knowing the valuable assets and insuring them in the enterprise-wide risk assessments.

2) Establish clearly documented and consistently enforced polices and controls. One of the causes of insider threats is when employees feel that they are treated differently when it comes to enforcement policies. Having policies in place, even without enforcing them, is better than not having policies at all. Policies are not documented to comply with audits, but are rather enforced to assure security. Failing to enforce policies and controls with clear documentation has resulted in insider attacks in the past [6].

3) Institute periodic security awareness training for all employees. Security awareness training is essential to inform employees about the existence of the organization's policies and to provide awareness that these policies need to be enforced. Using a security awareness program alerts employees about the consequences of not complying with the company's security policies.

4) Monitor and respond to suspicious or disruptive behavior, beginning with the hiring process. As detailed in the CERT Insider

Threat Database, most insider attacks started with multiple policy violations and aggressive behavior incidents that were ignored [6].

5) Anticipate and manage negative workplace issues. The workplace needs to be sufficiently healthy to encourage employees to be conscientious and productive. Any unmanaged negative workplace issues starting from pre-employment, where polices and consequences of violations are not communicated, to daily issues such as inappropriate relationships among workers, can cause an organization to be at risk from insiders. Most insider threats resulted from unmanaged negative workplace issues.

6) Track and secure the physical environment. As much as system security is essential to secure a business, physical security plays an important role that is often overlooked. Not all employees should gain access to all facilities in an organization, especially former employees. Attempts of access should always be logged to investigate the likelihood of physical security-related attacks.

7) Implement strict password and account management policies and practices. Password and account management are essential in securing an organization against insider threats. An anonymous form for reporting attempts of account violations can be used to protect those who report them. Any account that is not of use or belongs to a fired employee needs to be disabled. Periodic account auditing needs to be implemented to assure the legitimate use of user accounts.

8) Enforce separation of duties and least privilege principles. Separation of duties assures that insider attacks cannot be executed by a single insider working alone. Separation of duties also needs to be complemented with the principle of least privilege, which states that an employee is only granted the necessary privileges to perform his or her job. Enforcement of the separation of duties and least privilege principles reduces the risk of insider threats.

9) Consider insider threats during the software development life cycle (SDLC). Malicious code inserted while software is being developed

is a common insider threat. Addressing insider threats in the SDLC can be accomplished by performing code auditing, which is an important step before commissioning software into production. A change management system, in which each change is reviewed and approved before being integrated into the production software, is another control mechanism that can address SDLC-related insider threats.

10) Use extra caution with systems administrators and technical or privileged users. Systems administrators and privileged users have the capability to cause damages to the most valuable parts of an organization. Given their roles and privileges, they know how to mount attacks and cover their tracks. Separation of duties in critical functions may be a solution to deter privileged users from turning into malicious insiders, yet it is an insufficient measure by itself.

11) Log, monitor, and audit employees' online actions. Logs are essential to investigate a user's activity. These allow for a non-authorized activity to be identified and reported. Monitoring logs can be a daunting task, as log files may become very large. Solutions exist that filter logs based on pre-defined categories, and can assist in detecting insider threat cases.

12) Use layered defenses. The use of security awareness, logs, and employee monitoring, among other best practices as listed above, is important to mitigate insider threats. Using a single solution is usually not effective by itself in defending against insider threats, and it is always better to use multiple, layered solutions.

13) Deactivate computer access immediately after employment termination. Most insider threat attacks are the result of employees' accounts remaining active after employment termination. Therefore, deactivating access accounts may reduce an organization's risks related to insider threats.

14) Implement secure backup and recovery processes. Backups and recovery processes are important measures to assure business continuity in cases of insider threats. Therefore, it is important that

an organization implement a plan for secure backups, as well as data and service recovery.

15) Develop an insider incident response plan. Such a plan is essential to respond to any incident in a proper and effective manner. Evidence of an attack, who committed it, and how it was committed, are all necessary components of information that can help in mitigating similar attacks in the future. The incident response plan should also include the methods and steps to repair damage caused by an insider, with a specific concentration on the organization's most valuable services and resources.

Note that although all of the above best practices methods are useful, most of them are not technical controls, but rather controls related to management and human resources (HR). Our approach to preventing insider threats may support Best Practice #4 (monitoring and responding to suspicious or disruptive behavior), and can provide a filter aspect to Best Practice #11 (logging, monitoring, and auditing employees' online actions). However, we mainly focus on monitoring the physiological signals of the insider, as opposed to current controls that monitor behavioral signals, which controls are easy to fool.

2.1.5   Existing Solutions to the Insider Threat and Their Limitations

The US Department of Defense (DoD) Insiders Threat Integrated Process Team (IPT) indicates that "the internal security threat has existed for centuries and is even more serious than the external security threat because the potential perpetrator of malicious activity is authorized access" [7]. Today, due to the increase of digitized assets and the ease of compromising them, the threat of an insider has evolved and the related impact has risen. An organization's trust in an insider increases over time, causing what is known as the *trust trap*, where an insider gains privileges that may be used against the organization. As the user's privileges and trust continue to increase, the risk of insider threat increases, as well. Best practices are released periodically, such as the Common Sense Guide to Mitigating Insider Threats [8], which provides the practices and standards companies need to implement in order to mitigate insider threats. Yet, as per the 2013

State of Cybercrime Survey from PricewaterhouseCoopers (PwC) and CSO magazine [9], companies do not do enough to protect themselves from insider threats. The survey states that insiders are more likely to cause more serious damage to an organization than external attacks. Among companies who suffered insider attacks, 33% did not have an insider threat response plan, even though these plans have been suggested as a best practice for over a decade (since 2001) [10]. Some of the existing solutions to insider threats include implementing security awareness programs, data loss prevention, segregation of duties and least privilege, honeytokens, and finally, behavioral monitoring. The details of each technique and its associated limitations are presented as follows:

1) Security Awareness Programs

A security awareness program informs and educates employees about the importance of security. It provides them with the knowledge to safeguard the organization's assets and valuable resources that are under their control. It minimizes the lack of knowledge about potential threats and therefore limits the possibility of unintentional mistakes. It also decreases the potential of phishing attacks, in which an outsider uses an employee inside the company to launch an attack without the insider knowing it. Finally, it reduces the risk of insider threats by announcing the existence of security technology that monitors the users' activities and therefore can pinpoint criminals.

A security awareness program is necessary; however, it is not sufficient by itself. The limitation of the security awareness approach relies on the trust that is given to employees after educating them. For example, security awareness programs inform users about the importance of reporting suspicious behavior and the possibility of the existence of malicious insiders. However, people often do not report crimes for various reasons, such as fear of being considered a party to it, feeling that it is not important to report it, assuming that others have already reported it, and so on. The General Social Survey on Victimization shows that only two-thirds of witnessed crimes are reported [11].

2) Data Loss Prevention

Data Loss Prevention (DLP) is an important mechanism that ensures that private and secure data always remain secure and are never released without proper authorization. Related methods include preventing file copying to external memory spaces, and preventing the sending of sensitive data via email. Other methods include monitoring endpoints and network traffic. DLP requires that every piece of data to be classified based on its sensitivity level. It ensures that data at rest and in transit are not shared with unauthorized entities.

The limitation in DLP is that it mainly monitors information leakage, and that encryption algorithms can be used to overcome this constraint. Also, DLP administrators may themselves be the source of the threat.

3) Segregation of Duties and Least Privilege

Segregation of duties (SoD) limits the possibility of an individual working alone abusing his or her privileges. It ensures that at least two entities agree on a certain action, thus forcing an insider to risk finding an associate. Similarly, enforcing the least privilege (LP) principle assures that employees are given only the privileges required to perform their jobs. It is often a common practice to implement SoD and LP in an organization.

The limitation of SoD is that it does not prevent an organized crime in which more than one entity is involved. Also, LP does not prevent the abuse of the least privileges. A system administrator's least privilege abuse may still result in a catastrophic damage.

4) Honeytokens

Honeytokens are based on the idea that accessing a large number of files or a large volume of data is usually not common in any environment, and should trigger an alarm of possible misuse or an insider threat. The limitation in honeytoken technology is, however, the assumption that the access amount is equal to the risk level. This assumption results in a high level of false positives as well as false negatives. A malicious insider can access data in low amounts for a long period of time. Also, data encryption prevents honeytokens from detecting such activity, as encrypted documents are not comparable to documents that are included on the watch list.

Recent research work in the insider threat area includes system-level user behavior biometric analysis using Fisher features and Gaussian mixture to detect behavior abnormalities [12]. This research achieves a malicious insider detection accuracy of 80%. Other research involves monitoring computer activity [13]. This work uses anomaly detection algorithms to identify insider threats. Another area of research targets the detection of a malicious insider from the network layer. The authors in [14] used a Bayesian network model for predicting insider threats using a combination of covert channels and intrusion detection to report security events. A variety of other related work targets the host, network, or behavior monitoring, yet none targets the insider from a physiological perspective. Giving the catastrophic damages and the high risk involved with insider threats, there exists a need for a mechanism that detects, reports, and prevents an insider threat before it happens.

The measures described above, security awareness programs, DLP, LP, and honeytokens, are the most widely used in organizations and the most suggested insider threat prevention techniques to be implemented. However, there still exist another two measurements that provide better opportunities for preventing insider threats: 1) the monitoring of behavior, and 2) the monitoring of physiological signals. These measurements are discussed in Sections 2.3.1.1 and 2.3.1.2, respectively. However, it is worth noting that multiple approaches have been suggested to detect and prevent insider threats in different case scenarios, yet it becomes impractical when trying to implement measures based on individual cases. This makes it important to find a general approach for insider threat detection and prevention.

2.2   Identity-based Access Control

Trust is an important concept in human relationships. The theory of organizational identity and trust states that trust is developed by the identification level, while identification is affected by the organizational identity [iv]. However, in security, blind trust implies a threat to the protected assets. As an example, the concept of the trust trap states a significant effect on organization, as trust "increases over time, yielding a false sense of security because the trust leads to decreased vigilance toward the threat" [15].

Access control models rely heavily on identification via numerous authentication techniques, including passwords, tokens, and biometrics. Multi-modal and multi-factor authentication systems are also used in multiple environments. All these techniques are robust in granting authenticated and authorized individuals the assigned permissions and so are robust in preventing the outsider threat; however, none of the access control models addresses insider threats. All existing access mechanisms work by enrolling users, storing a user's personally identifiable information (PII) into a system by generating a user's specific template, and then matching the user's newly-submitted data to check whether the user has already been enrolled in the past or not. The template generation and matching are related to an identity. However, the assumption that registered identity is equivalent to good intent in accessing a certain resource is a major vulnerability in current authentication methods.

Most existing authentication methods are either based on "something you know," such as a password; "something you have," such as smart cards, tokens, and certificates; or "something you are," such as biometrics [1]. None of these authentication methods provides a determination of good intent of access at the time of the access request. These authentication methods do not prevent an authorized entity from becoming a malicious insider. The main vulnerability with these methods is that a user who is trusted at the time of enrollment is trusted forever, or until his or her access privileges have been revoked. This trust relationship is fixed, as the key on which the trust was established is invariant (whether it is a password, a physical key, or a biometric factor). Even when using continuous authentication [16], the underlying factor to determine the trust in the user is always invariant. The elimination of assumptions of trust is accomplished by basing this trust decision on the real intents of the user when requesting access to a resource. This is better done by knowing what the user's intent is with the specific access request, and not by asking the user to present a static and unvarying token.

Access control models have been studied for over a decade and are still improving [17]. Applied models are being used in a variety of applications that include physical security situations that involve airports; organizations; and home access control to computer and systems access control.

Many access control models have been proposed and implemented in the literature, including Discretionary Access Control (DAC) and Non-Discretionary Access Control (NDAC), which is also referred to a Mandatory Access Control (MAC) [18]. DAC models, such as Capability-based and Access Control List-based (ACL-based), involve the decision of the object creator "owner" to determine who can access the object and what level of access is permitted. DAC is an owner-based access control model that works well in some deployments, but is not a robust model to address insider threats. Non-Discretionary Access Control models overcome the weaknesses in DAC models by allowing the access control decisions to be accomplished from the operating system layer. Such a model reduces the human error factor and makes the access control model much more efficient. MAC includes Rule-based and Lattice-based access controls that provide access permissions based on a set of rules that are predefined in the system. The most used access control model by organizations is Role-based Access Control (RBAC) [19,20], which sets permissions to entities based on their roles in the company. Other non-discretionary access control models have been proposed such as History-based Access Control (HBAC) [21], Attribute-based Access Control (ABAC) [22], Policy-based Access Control (PBAC) [23], and Context-based Access Control (CBAC) [24], to list a few. Most of these access control systems are static: Once an access policy is added and its permissions have been assigned, these permissions do not change unless certain modifications occur. This static approach allows for the risk of insider threats, as permissions do not get revoked, but in contrast, are accumulated in a way that the user's privileges become more substantial over time. The literature suggests the use of Non-Discretionary Access Control models as these decisions become increasingly computerized.

Presently, dynamic access control models exist to complement the need for the evolving and continuously changing structures of organizations. This is where Risk-Adaptive Access Control (RAdAC) [25] becomes relevant. RAdAC is a dynamic risk-based access control model that assesses risks based on the characteristics of people, characteristics of IT components, characteristics of objects, environmental factors, situational factors, and heuristics. Each of these assessment components is a challenge by itself. The National Institute of Standards and Technology (NIST) represents the challenge of characteristics of people as *"User Information – This is the source of any information RAdAC would need to assess the trustworthiness of the people involved in the access decision, such as identification and authentication information, and authorizations such as their security clearance. Since RAdAC will have to render access decisions for people that do not hold security clearances, other information will need to be available to use in the risk determination process to determine a level of risk associated with granting them access. What sort of information might be valuable to determining their trustworthiness? Could a mini background investigation be done online[?]"* [25]. In this book, we address the RAdAC requirements of human trustworthiness by proposing the usage of physiological signals to detect intentions of access to prevent insider threats.

A related work on providing intent-based access is done by Microsoft [26]. Based on the user' interaction with the intent-based access mechanism, the system determines which application is allowed to access the user's owned resources. Although the patent may be relevant to this book, it is a behavior-based mechanism and addresses outsider threats as opposed to insider threats.

The notion of identity-based access control depends on the nature of the authentication component. If the authentication component requires authenticating an identity, then it is identity-based. If it does not depend on authenticating an identity, then it is non-identity-based.

2.3 Intention and Motivation Detection

In criminal law, before guilt can be determined, three aspects need to be established. The three aspects are referred to with the acronym MOM, which stands for Means, Opportunity, and Motive.

Means is the ability of the individual to commit the crime; Opportunity is the existence of a chance for an individual to commit the crime, and Motive is the reason the individual felt the need to commit the crime. Only when the three aspects have been established, can an individual be determined to be guilty.

In this book, crime is the result of an insider threat, and the insider threat is a special case of all crimes. In this case, the Means aspect always exists in the insider threat context, as all insiders have the ability to commit the crime by abusing their privileges. The Opportunity also always exists, since an insider always has the chance to abuse his or her privileges. However, the Motive aspect is not easily proven to exist. The determination of what resource an individual is targeting is addressed in the intention detection component, and the motive aspect is addressed in the motivation detection component. Before stating related work in intent and motivation detection, information related to both aspects is provided below.

2.3.1 Intention Detection

Intent in criminal law is the mental purpose to perform an action that is prohibited. It states that intention is the decision to bring about a prohibited action. When someone plans his or her action, he or she becomes aware of the possible consequences. Some of those consequences may be prohibited. The decision to continue with the plan despite the consequences means that actions done are, to some extent, intentional.

Intention detection has been studied in many research areas, including neuroprosthetics, activity support, in the context of human and information security generally, and in the context of access control specifically [26, 31, 40]. The area of neuroprosthetics (the field of aiding patients in movement restoration) is the most widely studied research area, in which the intention of movement is detected by analyzing EEG and electromyogram (EMG) signals [27, 28, 29].

Activity support approaches target intention detection by observation. Nakauchi *et al.* [30] proposed human behavior detection using embedded sensors in a smart room. Sensors are placed on doors, drawers, chairs, and so on. The data collected from these sensors is sent to a main server for analysis. Behaviors were recognized from the external observations by recording the current status of objects, observed events, and the frequency of activities. The authors reported that the system was capable of detecting the behavior while studying, eating, arranging, and resting, based on analyzing the sequences of actions. An experiment run on 10 participants showed an accuracy rate of 93.7% with new system users.

The intention detection approaches are either observationally/behaviorally-based or physiologically based:

2.3.1.1 Observationally/Behaviorally-based Intention Detection

Behaviorally-based intention detection is divided in this section into two parts, namely: 1) Behavior that accompanies a malicious intent of access, and 2) Early signs of behavior that indicate the development of a malicious intent.

2.3.1.1.1 Detecting Behavior That Accompanies Malicious Intent of Access

A relevant research area that targets hostile intent for access control focuses on identifying deception using the analysis of vocal expressions. GK1 is a layered voice analysis (LVA) software application that is produced by Nemesysco and is used for access control [31]. The software producer claims that by answering three to five questions, intentions can be detected. However, Elkins *et al.* [32] argued that a deception detection solution that relies solely on one cue, such as voice, lacks the ability to detect individuals who are capable of voice control. The authors state that multiple sensors should be applied to collect data from various sources, such as heart rate, pupil dilation, and linguistic content, in order to reduce false positives and to eliminate false negatives.

Burgoon *et al.* [33] proposed an intention detection method for hostile actions by using deception detection in verbal and non-verbal communications. The authors stated that the presence of deception as an internal state will result in deceptive cues that raise suspicion. They map an intention to an internal state that results in a behavior. However, an internal state might result in many behaviors, and one behavior might be the result of many internal states, which results in a weakness in the proposed approach. The authors used the interpersonal deception theory (IDT) to map behavioral cues to profiles. They defined a threshold of suspicion or trust behavioral cues as their detection method. The inferred intent is the result of behavioral cues that elicit arousal level, power, pleasantness, and intensity, and that are compared to general and individual-specific expected behavioral profiles. To be accurate, the approach requires a large database of different profiles for behavior detection for the decision method. Any different behavioral approach of a hostile intent will result in a false negative. New hostile actions will then be logged and stored in the database in order to become a detection signature for future hostile actions. Because of its use of an observational behaviorally-based method, this approach varies between individuals, and any hostile intent holder can fool the system by either mimicking a good intention or approaching the hostile action differently.

Experimentation on real hostile intent situations is a challenge for researchers, as it is nearly impossible to mimic a real-world scenario of hostile intent that might cause harm to participants. The experimental design will not be as realistic as it should be to evaluate the proposed solution. Elkins *et al.* [32] stated that applying social psychology theory and communication to evoke real emotions, stress, and tension reduces this limitation of experimental design and makes the evaluation of proposed solutions acceptable.

Intention detection plays a role, as well, in identifying social and terrorist networks [34, 35, 36, 37, 38]. Vybornova *et al.* proposed a method for identifying social tension and intention detection on the basis of natural language semantic analysis [38]. The authors used language syntax and semantics with statistical processing to identify social tension. They also used the general laws of natural language, as well as general psychological, psycholinguistic, and sociological rules and trends, as the foundation of their method.

2.3.1.1.2 Detecting early signs of behavior that cause the development of a mal-intent

Often, malicious insiders show early warning signs of malicious intent, including a change in their method of communication, facial expressions, work progress, and other characteristics [6]. A suggestion in [6] states that since current security tools cannot detect insider threats, there is a need to rely on employees and managers to notice such changes and respond accordingly. However, according to [39], humans are not always efficient at detecting emotion in others or even within themselves, resulting in a failure in the detection of malicious intents, especially if the early warning signs of these intentions are the result of emotions that are well-hidden. Therefore, relying on managers and colleagues to detect malicious intent of access is not a robust approach.

Current behavior detection techniques show promising results, yet any behaviorally-based system can be circumvented by a new behavior profile that the system is not yet trained to detect, or by mimicking a normal behavior.

2.3.1.2 Physiologically-based Intention Detection

Physiology is the study of the organ systems in the body. Physiological signals are the signals generated by the bodily organs, such as signals that originate from the heart (electrocardiogram (ECG)) and brain (electroencephalogram (EEG)). It is also the study of the signals that result from muscle movement (electromyogram (EMG)), skin conductance, Galvinic Skin Response (GSR), body temperature, or any other bodily organ.

The main advantage of relying on physiological signals is that they are involuntary, meaning that they provide information about the body's reaction that is not always controllable. For instance, an individual is not capable of controlling his or her body temperature, skin conductance, or brain signals, to list a few. The usage of physiological signals to analyze the possibility of malicious intent to prevent insider threats is an interesting approach and lies at the heart of this book.

Research projects reported in the literature that uses physiological signals for access control include Future Attribute Screening Technology (FAST) [40], which relies heavily on behavioral and physiological signals to detect malicious intent in the form of pre-crime technology where a crime is prevented before it is committed. FAST focuses on detecting terrorist activities. It requires users to pass through gates and reply to questions while their behavioral and physiological signals are analyzed. Physiological and behavioral signals include thermal imaging, ECG, respiration, eye movement, and facial expressions. However, the FAST approach involves a number of limitations, including:

☐ The need of a specialized facility to interrogate a user.

☐ Detection is in the form of an interview and therefore detection time is not fast.

☐ The approach is not continuous, resulting in a risk of development of malicious intention after initial intent authentication.

☐ Success rate 78%.

It has been discussed in [41] that even if the accuracy rate of detecting terrorists is 99%, there still exists a false positive of 1% of individuals who are accused of being terrorists when they are not. Existing solutions for detecting insider threats do not eliminate the threat completely, given that most approaches target human behavior. FAST, the only physiologically-based system, does not use brain signals for intention detection. This lack is its weakest point, as the brain is considered the source of planning and intention.

Until now, there has not been any intention detection of access approach that uses the source of intention, which is the brain. However, advancements in sensing and micro-computing technologies has increased the capability of sensing physiological information in an unprecedented way. Many of these technologies have been used for intention detection based on human behavior, such as movement sensors that predict possible actions, facial and vocal expressions, eye movements, and many other activities that a person can easily falsify and hence fool the prediction system with. Additionally, these technologies are not sufficiently robust and can generate a large number of false negatives. Our approach is based on the involuntary physiological response toward stimuli, which signals are generated by the brain, and which are extremely difficult to voluntarily control. A related work is done by [42] which investigates the possibility of detecting agreement vs. disagreement intention using the EEG signals with presented sentences before participants stated their intentions. This shows promise in the ability in detecting intentions of access by analyzing the EEG signals. The authors reported 80.62% accuracy using the Support Vector Machine classifier on the FC2 EEG channel.

2.3.2 Motivation Detection

"According to the theory of reasoned action, a higher intention motivation [leads to being] *more likely to do so."* [43]

As discussed in this section, Means and Opportunity always exist in the case of insider threats; however, Motive is not easily proven to exist. Motive in criminal law is the reason and cause that pushes an individual to commit a wrongful act. Motivation can be extrinsic (outside factor of motivation) or intrinsic (self-motivation).

Motivation detection has been studied in [85] to distinguish between three groups, labeled as *Not Motivated* and *Highly Motivated*. The paper concludes that there exists a difference in the P300 brain signal's amplitude among the three groups, with a mean of $\mu = 4.89$ with no motivation and $\mu = 6.1$ with high motivation. The results indicate that motivation levels can be computed and that if a user is highly motivated, his or her brain signals are associated with a stronger signal than in those who are not motivated.

The next section provides information about brain-computer interfaces (BCI), EEG signals, event-related potentials (ERP), and the Concealed Information Test (CIT), all of which inform this study.

2.4 Brain-Computer Interface (BCI)

In 1875, a scientist by the name of Richard Caton reported in the British Medical Journal that animals with exposed cerebral hemispheres present electrical phenomena, but it was not until 1924 that Hans Berger recorded the first EEG signals from humans. An oscillatory activity in the brain was identified by Berger when analyzing EEG traces. He was able to identify Berger's wave (8–12 Hz), also known as the *alpha* wave. In 1970, the field of brain-computer interfaces (BCI) was initiated, which mainly targeted neuroprosthetics applications such as restoring impaired movement, hearing, and sight. In the mid-1990s and after experimenting on animals, the first neuroprosthetic devices implanted in humans were successfully tested.

Low-cost BCI-based interfaces for the gaming industry and recreational applications were introduced into the market in 2006 by Sony. In 2007, NeuroSky released the first dry sensor technology as a consumer-based EEG. Also, a device for video games that use EEG was developed by OCZ Technology in 2008. In 2009, Mattel and NeuroSky released Mindflex, which is a game that involves steering a ball through an obstacle course. Around the same period, Emotiv Systems released EPOC, a 14-channel EEG device that can detect 13 conscious states and 4 mental states. In 2009, intendiX was released onto the market. Using intendiX, a user can trigger an alarm, type on a keyboard matrix, and copy text into an e-mail using only brain signals [45]. In 2012, Neurowear produced Necomimi [44], cat-like ears that are controlled by NeuroSky, a brain-wave reader. In the same year, g.tec presented the Screen Overlay Control Interface (SOCI), a new intendiX module. SOCI allows users to play several games using their mind with an accuracy of 99% for detecting different brain signals [45]. Currently, EEG signal acquisition devices are available at low cost (~$75).

Brain waves are classified into different types depending on their frequency. Each wave type provides certain knowledge about the state of the brain.

Table 1 shows a comparison between the different waves in terms of frequency, generated location in the brain, and the implied mental tasks.

Table 1. Comparison of EEG waves

Brain Wave Type	Freq. (Hz)	Originating Location in the Brain	Mental State
Gamma	30–100	Somatosensory cortex	Two senses combined, during recognizing objects using short-term memory matching
Beta	13–30	Both hemispheres, In the frontal lobe	Thinking
Mu	8–13	Sensorimotor cortex	Alert, anxious thinking, active concentration, working, idle hands and arms
Alpha	8–13	Posterior regions, both hemispheres; High-amplitude waves	Relaxed, eyes closed
Theta	4–8	In locations not related to tasks at hand	Idling, actively trying to repress, a response or action, dreaming, imagining
Delta	< 4	In front regions, high-amplitude waves	Dreamless sleep, non- (Rapid Eye Movement) REM sleep, unconsciousness

EEG studies rely on the 10-20 standard system of electrode placement, which defines specific naming conventions for scalp regions where electrodes can be placed. The 10-20 naming indicates the percentage differences between the *nasion*, the bridge of the nose, and the closest electrode, as well as the *inion*, the back of the head, and the closest electrode to be 10%. It also specifies the percentage difference between each electrode to the nearest electrodes to be 20%. Scalp caps are currently available with defined locations of electrode placements with different electrode placement standards. The electrode naming convention specifies the name of the region and a number. For example, O1 and O2 are two electrodes placed on the occipital lobe on the back of the scalp, and F3 and F4 are two electrodes placed on the frontal lobe on the front of the scalp. Similarly, temporal lobe electrodes are marked with the letter T, and parietal lobe electrodes are marked with the letter P. Odd numbers represent the left hemisphere, and even numbers represent the right hemisphere. Electrode locations, as specified by the Emotiv EPOC, are AF3, AF4, F3, F4, F7, F8, FC5, FC6, P7, P8, T7, T8, O1, and O2 following the 10-20 standard of electrode placement.

2.4.1   Electroencephalogram   (EEG)   Robustness   in
Patterns of Individual Differences and Similarities

Over the last few years, EEG-based systems have become an area of interest to researchers in various domains including that of user authentication, in which the EEG signal was proposed as a biometric measure to identify people. The EEG signal was proposed due to the individuality of the signal and its robustness against circumvention [55]. Like every other biometric system, the performance of an EEG-based system is an important factor. Using various feature extraction and selection methods, the False Rejection Rate (FRR) and False Acceptance Rate (FAR) metrics have been showing very promising results that reached 0% [52]. So far, EEG as a biometric trait has shown some potential use either by integrating it with existing security solutions or by using it as a separate standalone authentication measure.

In [46], the authors discussed EEG, ECG, and electrodermal response (EDR) as future authentication and identification models. They also discussed the ease of ECG signal analyses compared with EEG. Bio-signals, and specifically EEG, are difficult to analyze due to the complexity of brain waves and outside interferences.

In Pass-thoughts research [47], the authors used the EEG signal to replace password typing, where the user is simply asked to "think" of the password in order to achieve authentication. This proposed method overcomes the weaknesses that current authentication techniques suffer from, including password guessing, misplaced tokens, and circumvented traditional physiological biometrics. Some of the drawbacks that have been identified by the authors included the non-pervasiveness of EEG equipment and the lack of feedback to the users during the authenticating process.

Abdullah *et al.* [48] discussed the possibility of an EEG-based biometric system using 4 or fewer electrodes. Their hypothesis is that although it is possible to use up to 61 electrodes, the increased number of electrodes does not necessarily lead to better results. To prove their hypothesis, the authors ran a number of experiments in which 10 male subjects participated with eyes closed and open during 5 sessions. An auto-regression (AR) model was used for feature extraction. Results showed a 96% classification rate for eyes open and 97% rate for eyes closed in the case of 4 electrodes, 90% and 95% with 2 electrodes, and 70% and 87% with only 1 electrode. The authors argued that with fewer electrodes and with specific electrode placement, a faster recognition rate can be achieved as a result of less processing. The authors pointed out that with fewer electrodes, users' acceptance tended to be higher due to shorter user preparation.

Moreover, in [49], the authors evaluated the feasibility of biometric authentication using EEG signals based on visual evoked potential (VEP), which is effortless to induce in subjects. The authors analyzed the brain wave patterns when showing an image to the intended subject, and used one classifier for each subject for recognition. The work is an enhancement of previous work performed by [51, 52 and 53], in which hard-to-induce imagined activities were used.

The authors in [50] proposed simple spectral features of EEG signals based on the distribution of spectra in the spectral variance and the non-dominant region of the spectrum, which makes continuous authentication realistic. The authors reported a 79% verification rate in their experiment, testing 23 users with only 1 electrode.

In another study, imagination of words starting with random letters, and right and left hand movement imagination were used as mental tasks performed by the subjects in the experiment [51]. The authors proposed using a statistical framework that uses the Maximum A Posteriori Model and Gaussian Mixture Models for user authentication. Also, the authors stated that specific mental tasks are more suitable when using EEG as a biometric measure to achieve authentication. The authors reported a 7.1% Equal Error Rate (EER). Their findings also included: 1) From the start phase, the performance of verification reduces over days when increasing temporal distance, and 2) The performance improves over 2 days of data training.

In [52], Palaniappan *et al.* were able to reduce false acceptance rate (FAR) and false rejection rate (FRR) with EEG-based biometric systems. In the study, channel spectral powers, auto-regression (AR) coefficients, non-linear complexity, inter-hemispheric channel linear complexity, and inter-hemispheric channel spectral power differences were used as features. The two stages for authentication were listed as imposter vs. client pattern recognition for the first stage. This stage guarantees a zero-valued FAR. Even though the FRR is expected to be very high, the second stage addresses this issue by detecting whether the subject is from the client category or the imposter category: if the subject is from the client category, the classification rate is compared against the set threshold for authentication. If the subject is from the imposter category, a second threshold is used. The employed activities for enrollment are baseline activity, where subjects are asked to relax while recording their brain signals, then asking them questions such as multiplication tasks, geometric figure rotation, letter composing activity, and visual counting activities. The authors stated that they reached zero-valued FAR and FRR when the method was tested on 5 subjects.

Unlike [51, 52], He *et al.* [53] proposed an authentication scheme that employs EEG hashing. Their approach is based on extracting features using multivariate-autoregressive (mAR) coefficients and then hashing them using the Fast Johnson-Lindenstrauss Transform (FJLT) algorithm. A probabilistic model known as Naïve Bayes is then used on the hashed values for authentication. EEG data were collected from 4 healthy subjects using 19 electrodes. The results showed an Equal Error Rate (EER) of 6.7%.

The authors in [54] suggested using EEG as a second factor of authentication combined with passwords. Their approach, called EEGPass, involves adding the mental state factor in pieces of a broken password. They claim that the resistance of the password to password cracking tools increased due to the addition of two aspects in each of the password's broken parts: namely, relaxation (beta wave) and attention (alpha wave) mental status.

In [55], the authors proposed new EEG features based on the convexity of spectral distribution with only one electrode and one channel for brain signal acquisition. The authors suggested using the *alpha* signal from one electrode to tackle the issue of high computational load of signal processing and feature extraction from many electrodes. The authors concluded that the power spectrum of the *alpha* signal is effective for personal authentication. The Equal Error Rate (EER) was found to be 11%, which is equivalent to similar studies of EEG signals for human authentication with fewer electrodes, shortened measuring time, reduced computational load, and higher user acceptance.

The above research shows the robustness of the usage of brain signals for user identification, which indicates the existence of unique signatures and patterns between individuals. There also exists a body of research that focuses on finding similarities between individuals' brain signals and the emotional state of a user.

Reliable computerized emotion detection has always been difficult to achieve as well as unreliable. Computerized methods for detecting emotion are limited to those traits in people that are observable, and often include changes or variations in those observable traits. These observable traits have included facial expressions [56], micro expressions [56], body language [57], speech patterns [58] and, more recently, brain pattern analysis or EEG signals [59].

Although an individual's brain patterns are not commonly observable, the introduction of brain-computer interface devices (BCIs) and the extensive research in this area in the last few years has made it increasingly practical for computers to reliably and accurately detect the emotional or affective state of an individual. The work discussed in [15] provides a scientific basis for the collection and analysis of brain pattern data to detect emotion. The work described in [24] validates the science of accurate emotion detection through EEG. The technology described in [25, 29] demonstrates the effective use of NeuroSky's MindSet EEG device, which accurately detects emotion through brainwave pattern analysis using only a single electrode.

The literature shows the robustness of the usage of brain signals for detecting similarities in multiple individuals' brain signals in terms of emotion detection; we believe that there may exist a pattern of similarities when an individual has malicious intent of access. Also, and most importantly in relation to this research, is identifying an identity not to grant access, but to detect an insider. Using EEG in order to detect intention of access provides us the ability to identify who requested access, as well. In this case, we determine an identity not to grant access but to log that identity with the access decision. A person with malicious intention of access, if identified, cannot deny being accurately identified.

The next section discusses a brain response that serves as a similarity measure among individuals.

2.4.2   Event-Related Potential (ERP)

The P300 brainwave (P3) is an event-related potential (ERP) that is a positive waveform that occurs 300 milliseconds after the onset of a stimulus (Figure 2-2). Such EEG reaction to stimuli demonstrates familiarity in the presented stimuli because a memory recall elicits P300 peaks [60]. P300 amplitude, which has a value of 2–10 μV, is sensitive to the extent of attention resources that are engaged, and P300 latency, which is approximately 250 ms to 500 ms, is sensitive to the amount of time required for recognition [61]. The P300 component latency changes across the scalp. It is longer over parietal areas, but shorter over frontal areas [62,63]. An example of a memory recall is showing a person an image of his or her home, which results in a P300 peak that is read when recording the EEG signals. Although the reaction is read from the EEG signals, raw EEG data still require extensive signal processing due to several sources of noise called artifacts. These artifacts originate from environmental factors such as cable noise and biological sources such as ECG, which are the heart signals, EMG, which are the electrical signals that result from the muscle movements, and the electrooculography (EOG), which are the electrical signals that result from blinking and eye movement.

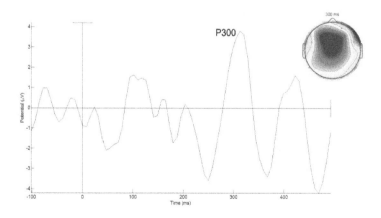

Figure 2-2. P300 peak.

Because P300 is best recorded in the central regions of the brain, the *Fz*, *Cz*, and *Pz* electrodes as seen in Figure 2-3 and the Emotiv EPOC electrode locations do not cover the best-known locations from where P300 is evoked, Ekanayake [64] investigated Emotiv EPOC's validity of capturing real EEG data and detecting P300 peaks. In the three sessions of the experiment, Ekanayake found that clear ERP waveforms were recognized. The clarity of ERP waveforms increases when the number of epochs becomes large. Moreover, Ekanayake found that P300 is best observed from electrodes placed in P7 and O1 locations, as the clarity decreases at locations P8, O2, FC5, F3, and F4. Regarding the other locations of the Emotiv EPOC device, no other ERP waves were found. He concluded by confirming the Emotiv EPOC's capability to capture P300 and subsequently real EEG data.

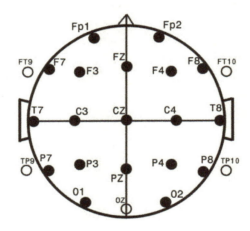

Figure 2-3. *Fz*, *Cz*, *Pz* electrodes locations

[65].

For better P300 analysis, a study done by Krusienski *et al.* [66] evaluated the performance of five P300 classification methods: a nonlinear method known as Gaussian kernel support vector machine (GSVM) and four linear methods known as Fisher's Linear Discriminant (FLD), Pearson's Correlation Method (PCM), Linear Support Vector Machine (LSVM), and Stepwise Linear Discriminant Analysis (SWLDA). The tested methods were applied on data that had been collected using the P300 Speller paradigm. The data were collected from eight subjects for classification. Although all tested methods showed an acceptable performance level, results indicate that FLD and SWLDA achieved the best performance to classify P300 Speller data among all of the methods tested.

There exist multiple sources of publicly available P300 data sets, such as those provided in BCI Competitions I, II and III [67]. The BCI challenge provides datasets in order for the research community to compete on processing signals and to achieve improved classification. BCI P300 data sets have been used by [68], and classification accuracy reached 96.5% on a test set that had 200 spelling characters using an SVM classifier. An accuracy using the BCI competition's P300 data reached 100% in both [69, 70] using SVM and wavelet decomposition, respectively.

The next section discusses the robustness of using P300 signals as a measurement of detection of concealed information.

2.4.3   Concealed Information Test (CIT) Using P300-

The Concealed Information Test (CIT), formally referred to as the Guilty-Knowledge Test, is a test that aims to detect the existence or absence of crime-related information in an individual's memory. CIT is performed by asking suspects specific questions about details related to a crime that only the criminal would know (e.g., was the stolen item a hard disk, a monitor, or a flash drive?). The crime-related details are commonly referred to as *probes* (Targets), and the similar class possible-crime details are commonly referred to as *irrelevant* (Non-Targets). An innocent would not differentiate between the probes and the irrelevant items, yet a criminal would show a difference. When a suspect answers the questions, his or her physiological signals are recorded. Only the answers that a suspect knows would result in a different physiological response (P300). By analyzing the responses of each subject, only criminals show reactions to related crime details (probes). CIT has been reported to be the most validated test for concealed information [71, 72, 73]. The commonly used CIT physiological signals are Galvanic Skin Response (GSR), heart rate (HR), and EEG, among others. It has been reported that the accuracy of detection of concealed information ranges from 70–90% [72]. However, an advancement of the P300-based CIT accuracy of correct detection has been reported that includes the use of the Complex Trial Protocol (CTP), a countermeasure-resistant protocol, with an accuracy of correct detection of 90% to 100% [79].

2.4.3.1   Accuracy of P300-based CIT

Many researchers conducted research using CIT for the detection of past crime-related details [71, 72, 73, 74, 75, 76]. Farwell [74, 75] used P300 as a brain fingerprinting measure. Farwell stated that the use of P300 is a valid approach to detect information that resides in the brain by showing textual or visual stimuli. His approach, known as Memory and Encoding Related Multifaceted Electroencephalographic Response (MERMER), is based on showing three types of stimuli, namely: irrelevant, which is general information that is not relevant to the investigated incident; target, which is information that the subject knows; and probes, which is information that only the investigator knows and the subject denies knowing. If probes and target stimuli show P300 peaks, then recognition of information has been achieved. Brain fingerprinting is an approach that is used to detect the existence of information that is due to past experiences. Farwell stated that brain fingerprinting is limited only to the recognition of information, but is not capable of detecting why this information is recognized. Brain fingerprinting is currently used for criminal investigations and has been accepted in courts of law (e.g., the case of Harrington v. State [76]).

Just as the detection of past crime is important to convict criminals for what they have done, the concept of pre-crime detection becomes essential to prevent crimes from happening. It has been shown that the analysis of criminals' brain signals can be used to predict the likelihood of their committing a crime again after being released. The authors in [77] used magnetic resonance imaging (MRI) for their study. They analyzed the anterior cingulate cortex of the brain, which is responsible for "error processing, conflict monitoring, response selection, and avoidance learning" [77]. The authors state that some of the inmates show parts of their "brain that might not be working correctly which gives us a look into who is more likely to have an anti-social behavior that leads to re-arrest" [77]. The above work provides insights into the fact that the detection of pre-crime is possible.

The P300-based CIT for crime-related details has reported an accuracy rate of correct detection that ranges between 70%-100% accuracy [78]. From the P300-based CIT perspective of pre-crime, Meixner *et al.* [79] were able to detect the existence of terrorists' future plans by applying CIT with a proof of the robustness of using P300, to detect the existence of future terrorist plans. The authors have run an experiment on 24 participants divided in two equal groups: one group planning a terrorist attack and another group planning a vacation. The terrorist group was tested on three pieces of concealed information: knowledge of location, method, and time. By stimulating the participants' brains with text of two categories, 1) Target that represents the location, method, and time of the terrorist attack, and 2) Non-target that represents general locations, times, and methods, the authors achieved 100% correct classification of terrorists and innocents. The result of the experiment showed that the terrorist group resulted in a P300 peak to those target texts enabling detection of 12/12 of the terrorist group with no false positives out of 24 suspects, 12 of which were innocents. The authors suggest that this protocol has the potential to detect future terrorist activity; however, the approach is not suitable for access control as it requires over 25 minutes of stimuli presenting time. Furthermore, the authors' protocol required subjects to practice for 5 minutes which is not realistic in real-world scenarios and questions their results. The authors requested subjects to respond to a visual stimulus which presents a weakness in the approach as the approach requires the cooperation from the subject to detect their plan.

In the next chapter, the adaptation a P300-based CIT approach in order to detect intents of access and build Intent-based Access Control to prevent insider threats is provided.

2.5   Conclusion

Governments, organizations and companies invest money, effort, and time in order to mitigate insider threats; however, existing access control solutions fail to do so, as they derive trust from identity. The current solutions do not prevent insider threats mainly because they rely on static factors or behavioral aspects that can be easily circumvented. Reliance on uncontrollable physiological measures results in a better solution for the insider threat, as it targets the insider's uncontrollable responses. The P300-based CIT method shows promising results for the detection of concealed information, and we adopt and adapt this approach to test the potential of Intent-Based Access Control (IBAC) in preventing insider threats. The next chapter discusses the research objectives and methodology required to address the insider threat problem, mainly by relying on the insider's uncontrollable physiological signals.

CHAPTER 3. Research Objectives and Methodology

3.1 Overview

Given the costly damages and the high risk involved with insider threats, there exists a need for a mechanism that minimizes this problem. Although a number of approaches to detect and prevent insider threats exist [10], any measurement that does not proactively prevent new attacks would be accompanied by high risk and would leave protected resources vulnerable. Any measurement for detecting insider threats should not rely on:

1) **Human involvement.** People often do not report crime for various reasons, such as fear of being accused of being part of it, feeling that it is not important to report it, assuming that others have already reported it, and so on. The General Social Survey on Victimization shows that only two-thirds of witnessed crime is reported [80]. While it is always important to have mechanisms in place to allow people to report crime-related behavior, including the knowledge of an insider incident, the success of the mechanism should not ultimately rely merely on human actions.

2) **Determining or identifying an identity**. Current access control systems rely heavily on the identity aspect and relate identity to trust and intentions of access. However, as discussed in Section 2.2, the main reason why insider threats exist is due to the assumption that identity is equivalent to good intentions.

3) **Controlled behavior**. Any reliance on signatures that result from controlled behavior cannot provide protection from insider threats. An example is given in Section 2.3.1.1 in Nemesysco GK1 system that claims to detect malicious intent by relying only on voice, where voice-capable

individuals are able to deceive the system.

We supplement Jackson's [2] recommendation of combining computer science with psychology in order to predict insider threats from the behavioral perspective by suggesting the combination of computer science with cognitive psychology, where the insider thinks, reasons, intends, plans, and acts.

We target the insider threat from the access control layer, since access control is the first layer of defense, especially as it directly interacts with insiders. We identify the vulnerability in access control models and propose a solution that mainly relies on:

a) The theory of identity and trust that suggests that trust should not be based on identity, which serves as the base of the common vulnerability in existing access control models [iv].

b) Planned behavior theory and, specifically, intention detection that serves as the proposed solution for insider threats, where we detect the user's intention of access as opposed to detecting his or her identity.

c) Brain-computer interface (BCI) technology and, specifically, P300-based CIT that serves as the adopted and adapted approach for intention detection. P300-based CIT provides information about the existence of knowledge about an intention that we exploit to detect the intention of the access request. It also provides information about the motivation levels related to an intention that we propose to use in order to detect the likelihood of intention execution, which influences the access risk level. P300-based CIT and intention detection theories serve as the core components of the IBAC system.

This chapter provides clarifications of the research objectives in Section 3.2, and describes in Section 3.3 the methodological approaches to address the stated research challenges.

3.2 Research Objectives

As opposed to previously proposed mechanisms that require human intervention [40], determining or verifying an identity, or measuring a control behavior [31,38], in order to tackle insider threats, we propose that effective measurements may rely on:

1) **Involuntary Measurements.** Any measurement that a human does not have control over and that provides a clear distinction between malicious intent and good intent would be of use.

2) **Automatic Measurements.** Any measurements should be automatic and not rely on human interaction.

In order to fulfill the above requirements and provide a solution for insider threats, we developed the following quantitative research objectives in support of the research hypotheses:

Main Objective: To study the potential of using Intent-based Access Control (IBAC) in detecting and preventing malicious insiders.

We investigate the potential of using IBAC in detecting and preventing insider threats by determining whether to grant or deny access to protected resources regardless of the identity. In order to address the main objective, the research is developed with the following supporting objectives:

Objective 1 : To detect intentions of access.

    a. To adopt and adapt P300-based CIT to accurately detect intentions of access using involuntary physiological signals.

    b. To exploit an individual's self-knowledge about an intention using P300-based CIT.

Objective 2 : To detect motivation levels.

a. To detect the motivation level of access using the P300 signal amplitude that corresponds to the detected intention.

The above objectives deliver the intention category and the probability of execution (motivation), and serve as the two inputs to calculate the access risk level. Also, the above objectives address the possibility of intention detection (Hypothesis 1) and motivation detection (Hypothesis 2), which are the two main components of the IBAC system.

Objective 3 : To design the Intent-based Access Control (IBAC) model and calculate the total access risk.

a. To design the IBAC system.

b. To incorporate the detected intention category with the detected motivation level along with the requested asset value.

i. To assess the IBAC system while granting or denying access based on the calculated risk.

Objective 4 : To report the potential of Intent-based Access Control (IBAC) in detecting and preventing insider threats.

a. To test if IBAC is capable of granting access to individuals with less risk, but denying access to individuals with high risk using their intention, motivation, and the corresponding requested asset value.

Objective 3 provides the design and results of the system to evaluate the ability to combat insider threats. Objective 4 investigates the potential for detecting and preventing insider threats, which in return provides the Main Objective of studying the potential of IBAC in preventing insider threats (Main Hypothesis).

The rationales of the objectives originate from the fact that intentions are mainly future plans, and an access control model that prevents access based on future plans (intentions) would reduce the risk of insiders, as opposed to existing access control models that rely only on identity. In this case, IBAC serves as a non-identity-based access control model that prevents malicious insiders from gaining access to protected resources.

Figure 3-1 depicts the objectives and how they are combined to answer the research questions. The next section describes the research methodology employed to address these research objectives.

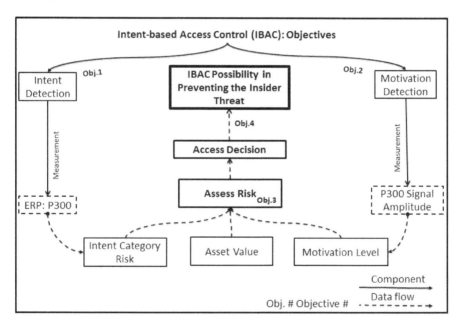

Figure 3-1. Intent-based Access Control (IBAC) objectives

3.3 Methodology

Since the research problem of insider threats is related to humans, human experimentation is necessarily the elected experimental method. In this section, each objective is addressed within a subsection to fairly provide the best proposed method to achieve it.

Main Objective: To study the potential of using Intent-based Access Control (IBAC) to detect and prevent malicious insiders.

According to [81], the Fogg Behavior Model (FDM) "asserts that for a target behavior to happen, [an intention being executed], a person must have sufficient motivation, sufficient ability and an effective trigger" [81], as depicted in Figure 3-2. The model states that the probability of a target behavior to be performed depends on the motivation level and the ability level of the potential perpetrator. Since all insiders have high ability to abuse their privileges, the condition of sufficient ability is always met. In the insider threat case, motivation is the only measurement that predicts the likelihood of an intent being executed, as depicted in Figure 3-3. An effective trigger occurs when an intention exists and access is granted, and with sufficient motivation, the target behavior is performed.

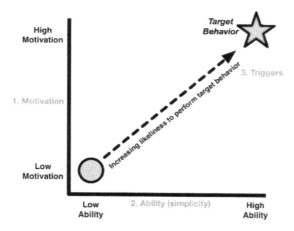

Figure 3-2. Motivation, ability levels and the likelihood of executing a target behavior(intention)

[81].

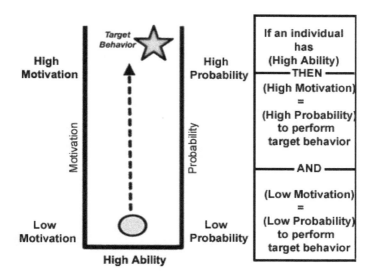

Figure 3-3. Motivation and probability levels to execute a target behavior in the insider threat context.

Therefore, intention and motivation detection are essential in addressing the main objective. Thus, we address the 4 objectives of this work first. In order to test the potential of IBAC in preventing insider threats, we provide in this section the methodology for the 4 main components. The 4 components are intention detection of access; the probability of an intention to be executed (motivation); the IBAC design and risk calculation; and the access decision, which are provided in Sections 3.3.1, 3.3.2, 3.3.3, and 3.3.4 respectively. Each section addresses a research objective, from **Objective 1** to **Objective 4**, and provides the proposed approach to achieve this objective.

3.3.1 Intention Detection

Intentions, as explained in Section 2.3, are driven by intrinsic or extrinsic agents, where an intention of an action becomes a future plan and where a plan imminent (occurring within a matter of seconds) or far in the future (occurring within a matter of days or weeks). Because intentions are mainly future plans, and because an individual possesses knowledge about their intention, we hypothesize that it is possible to exploit the self-knowledge an individual has about an intention of theirs before that intention is executed using brain-computer interface (BCI) technology generally, and using P300-based Concealed Information Test (CIT) specifically.

The proposed BCI approach uses EEG signals, which are the electrical signals that result from neurons firing in the brain, to determine the actual intentions of the user. EEG has shown great potential as a strong and robust channel of information retrieval, as well as a biometric authentication measure [82, 83, 84]. To detect a user's intentions, we propose the usage of non-invasive physiological signals of the brain that are generated in response to pre-determined stimuli. Based on the non-invasive acquisition of users' physiological signals, we test in a laboratory setting the possibility of using the P300 signal, a positive electrical brainwave spike that occurs 300 ms after a recognition of an intention and that the human brain emits involuntarily, as an intention detection measure.

With the robustness of using P300-based CIT on the detection of concealed information as presented in Section 2.4.3, we aim in this study to adopt and adapt the P300-based CIT in order to detect intent of access as a specific case of concealed information, in order to test the possibility of the first component of the Intent-based Access Control (IBAC) model, which is intention detection.

In order to achieve Objective 1, which aims "to detect intentions of access," we designed two experiments. The first experiment is intended to detect an extrinsically-based intention, which is an intention we impose on participants to have, among possible intentions that participants do not know we test for. The second experiment is intended to detect an intrinsically-based intention, which is an intention that participants choose to have, among possible known intentions, without informing us about what intention they have. Details of each experiment are provided in Chapter 4, Experimental Design to Determine the Potential of IBAC.

3.3.2   Motivation Detection

Motivation, as explained in Section 2.3, is the reason and cause that pushes an individual to commit a wrongful act. According to [81], if an individual has a high motivation and a high ability, the probability of an intention being executed is high. Also, according to the theory of reasoned action, "a higher intention motivation [leads to being] more likely to do so" [43]. In the IBAC system, motivation plays an important role in assessing the risk of access; therefore, it is important to find a suitable solution to detect motivation levels.

We hypothesize that motivation levels can be detected by analyzing the P300 signal amplitude that occurs when an intention is recognized and detected. This provides a single measurement, P300, for intent detection and motivation detection, and focuses the detected motivation level to the specific detected intention.

It has been shown that motivation determines the P300 amplitude [85]. Kleih *et al.* ran an experiment on three groups of participants; one with no motivation and two with different levels of motivation. The group motivation levels were determined based on the amount of money paid to participants to pay attention to detecting specific information. The research work shows that if motivation is high, participants pay high attention, that results in an increased P300 amplitude, towards detecting information, and vice versa. Figure 3-4 depicts the trend that the level of attention devoted to detecting information is a result of motivation level. Therefore, if motivation is high, participants pay more attention to the information. Also, if motivation is low, participants pay less attention to the information.

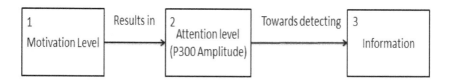

Figure 3-4. The relationship between motivation level, attention level, and information.

We hypothesize that the inverse relationship between motivation and attention is correct, as well, in the context of motivation toward intention; i.e., the P300 amplitude is a determination of the motivation level. The inverse relationship that we hypothesize is that when we present information to participants that relates to a concealed piece of information about an intention that they intend to execute, participants will pay more attention, and consequently have a higher P300 amplitude, compared with presenting information to participants that relates to concealed information about an intention that they do not intend to execute. Figure 3-5 depicts the relationship between motivation level, attention level, and information in detecting motivation level by presenting information to elicit attention. The inverse relationship states that depending on the level of concealed information of intention that is presented to participants who have them, attention level increases or decreases, and motivation level is then detected. If participants are shown information about an intention that they are motivated to execute, they devote more attention to it, compared with showing participants information about an intention they are not motivated to do. In this way, attention level corresponds to the motivation level and since the P300 amplitude is a measurement of attention, we conclude that the P300 amplitude corresponds to the motivation level.

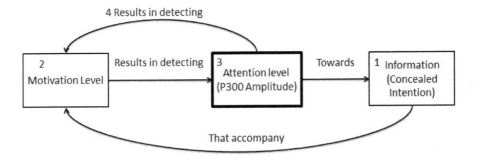

Figure 3-5. The inverse relationship between motivation level, attention level, and information in detecting motivation by presenting information.

3.3.3 Intent-based Access Control (IBAC) Design

Now that the first two objectives have been addressed, and in order to calculate the total access risk level (**Objective 3**), we designed the access control elements. IBAC design is provided in Section 3.3.3.1.

IBAC is an access control model that grants or denies access based on the risk that is computed when detecting the intentions and motivations of users. It is based on the current measurements of the physiological signals that users emit involuntarily at the time of an access request. The physiological signals allow the determination of the intent of the user and hence form a decision about what level of access should be granted. Users' intentions are not binary, and the various types and levels of intentions and motivations are used in a formula to calculate a risk level and therefore a variable level of access. Currently, only two levels of access are used to grant or deny access, but based on the calculated risk, various levels can be introduced, such as grant with high level of access, grant with low level of access, or deny access.

An intention is defined as making an explicit conscious decision to perform an action. Intentions are deliberate, and forming one is an automatic process unless it is revised. An intention leads an agent to perform the action directly. Intentions have stability, and once formed, an intention has a tendency to persist [86]. Because of this, a reaction to a stimulus that presents a view of the intended action would reveal that intention by showing a P300 spike, which indicates recognition of the intended action. IBAC is an access control system that detects the intentions of access. Therefore, it is tested to determine whether it has the potential to deny access to those who show malicious intent and grants access to those whose brain signal shows no evidence of a malicious intent. The IBAC design is provided in the following section.

3.3.3.1   IBAC Design

IBAC is a risk-based, rather than an identity-based, access control model that measures risk based on the intention of access and the motivation levels. IBAC works based on three components: 1) Intent and Motivation Detection, 2) Risk Assessment, and 3) Access Decision. Risk Assessment relies on the Intent Detection component, and Access Decision relies on the Risk Assessment component. The IBAC components are described in more detail in the following:

1)   Intent and Motivation Detection (IMD)

The Intention and Motivation Detection (IMD) component receives input from non-invasive sensors that are attached to the user's head. Once the physiological signals are obtained, they are filtered, classified, and analyzed to detect the intention and the level of that intention (motivation level).

IMD returns the intention category that is detected from a set of possible intentions. Each intent category is assigned a value that influences the overall risk. The intent category value assignment depends on the resources that the system is protecting and, as such, assigning the impact value of an intent is the organization's decision. IMD also returns the motivation level which corresponds to the likelihood of an intent being executed.

2)   Risk Assessment (RA)

Risk is defined as the probability of a threat exploiting a vulnerability in an asset. Three components exist in the definition of risk: threat, vulnerability, and asset. In this book, the threat and the vulnerability always exist. The threat is the insider threat, and the vulnerability is the abuse of privileges causing damage to assets.

The RA component provides an assessment of risk levels associated with the type of intention to exploit a vulnerability in an asset and the motivation level (Probability) with regard to the value of the asset that is protected. The RA component calculates a risk level and then passes the results to the Access Decision component.

Once an intention is detected, the intention category cost value that corresponds to the detected intention is assigned in the Intent Category (*IntC*), which is provided by the asset owner.

Because intentions are highly driven by the motivation level that accompanies the tested intention [43, 81], the motivation level, which is a factor that influences an individual to commit an intended action, is used to determine the probability of an intention being executed. Therefore, the Intention Motivation (*IntM*) value is assigned to the IntM, which is determined by the P300 amplitude and is computed as follows:

$$Intention\ Motivation \triangleq Amplitude(P300)$$

(1)

The risk assessment theory [87, 88, 89] states that risk is equal to *Loss* x *Probability* of occurrence. The following equation calculates the total risk level as defined by the risk assessment theory which states that risk is equal to the impact multiplied with the probability of impact. Since the impact in the insider threat context is the intention and the probability of the impact is the motivation level towards the intention the risk value is calculated as follows:

Risk (*R*) is the total risk and is defined as:

$$R = \frac{(Motivation\ level * Intention\ category\ value)}{100}$$

(2)

Motivation levels are assigned values between 0 and 1, since motivation functions as the probability. The intention category value is to be assigned values between 0 and 100. The motivation levels are detected by the P300 amplitude, and the intent category is detected by the Intention Detection component. In contrast, the intent category value is determined by the asset owner.

After calculating the total risk of a specific intention toward a particular asset with a specific motivation, we may provide an access decision based on the overall risk. However, basing the access decision on overall risk alone is misleading, as a low percentage risk may result in a wrong access decision unless the asset value is also taken into consideration. Therefore, the risk assessment component assesses risk as follows:

$$\textbf{Total Estimated Loss} = R * \textit{Asset value} \qquad (3)$$

The Total Estimated Loss is the value provided to the decision-making component to decide whether to deny or to permit access to protected assets.

If motivation level is 1 and the damage value on an asset if exploited (intent) is 100, then risk on asset will be $\frac{(1*100)}{100} = 1$ out of 1 risk if access is granted, which means that the probability of losing 100% of the value of the asset is 100%. The total possible loss as per equation (3) if the asset value is $\$1M = 1 * \$1M = \$1M$ loss.

If motivation level is 0.5 and the cost is 100, then total risk is $\frac{(0.5*100)}{100} = 0.5$ out of 1 risk if access is granted, which indicates the probability of losing half of the value of an asset. The total possible loss as per equation (3) if the asset value is $\$1M = 0.5 * \$1M = \$500K$.

3) Access Decision (AD)

The Access Decision (AD) component maps the Risk Assessment output to a decision about whether to grant or deny access to an asset. AD bases the decision on the estimated loss of value in an asset and the threshold of accepted value loss in an asset. For example, if $10K value is the threshold of accepted loss in an asset, any total estimated loss that is above that threshold would result in access being rejected, and any total estimated loss that is below that threshold would result in access being granted. The decision is to be determined by the organization deploying the system to deny or allow access. The organization will also determine levels of access, report incidents, raise flags, and/or monitor users.

Although IBAC has been described and illustrated in exemplary forms with a certain degree of specificity, it is noted that the description and illustrations have been made by way of example only. Numerous changes in the details of construction, and combination and arrangement of parts and steps, may be made. Except to the extent explicitly stated or inherent within the processes described, including any optional steps or components thereof, no required order, sequence, or combination is intended or implied. As will be understood by those skilled in the relevant arts, with respect to both processes and any systems, devices, etc., described herein, a wide range of variations and modifications are possible, and even advantageous, in various circumstances. IBAC is intended to encompass all such variations and modifications within its scope. Figure 3-6 shows a schematic diagram of the Intent-based Access Control system. It depicts the IBAC system flow starting from (2) to (9).

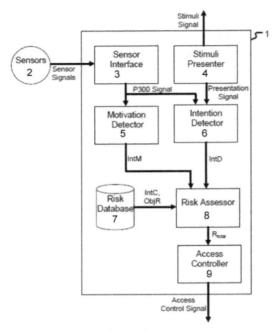

Figure 3-6. Schematic diagram of IBAC.

Figure 3-7 depicts the IBAC flow in detail. When a sensitive object access is requested, the EEG signals are acquired while intention-related images flash in front of the user. Signal pre-processing and processing are applied to the signal to detect the intention category and the motivation level. Additional information can be used to assess the risk, such as using data from an environmentally aware system, the user's role, and user history. Once the access risk has been calculated, the classifier determines whether access should be granted or rejected.

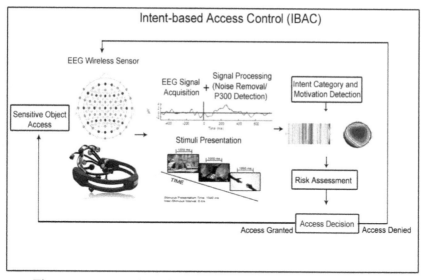

Figure 3-7. Intent-based Access Control (IBAC) design in detail.

3.3.4   Potential of IBAC in Preventing Insider Threats

To achieve Objective 4, to report the potential of IBAC in detecting and preventing insider threats, we achieve Objectives 1, 2 and 3, and then test whether IBAC is capable of granting access to individuals with less risk, but denying access to individuals with high risk using their intention, motivation, and the corresponding requested asset value. If IBAC shows the capability and the potential of preventing the insider threat, we report the accuracy of granting and denying access to users. This achieves the main objective, to study the potential of using Intent-based Access Control (IBAC) to detect and prevent malicious insiders.

The next chapter provides the experimental design to achieve Objective 1, detecting intentions of access, Objective 2, detecting motivation levels, Objective 3, calculating risk of access, and Objective 4, reporting the potential of IBAC in preventing insider threats. Chapter 5 provides the data analysis and results of each objective.

CHAPTER 4. Experimental Design to Determine the Potential of IBAC

4.1 Overview

This chapter provides the experimental design to test the potential of Intent-based Access Control (IBAC). We start by presenting two initial experiments that are conducted to test the capability of the Emotiv tool in detecting the P300 signal that is then used to test the possibility of detecting intention of movement direction. Next, the Emotiv tool is used in the two main experiments to test the hypotheses of the potential of IBAC in preventing the insider threat, followed by an extensive discussion. In Section 4.2, the experimental designs are provided including a description of each experimental goal, research subjects, procedures, procedure discussion, criteria for selection images and the test environment.

4.1.1 Initial Experiments

Two initial experiments have been designed and carried out with the objective of: 1) Testing the possibility of P300 detection using Emotiv EPOC, a wireless 14-channel EEG acquisition device, based on the possibility of using P300 Speller, and 2) Testing the possibility for detection of the intent of movement direction.

Experiment 0.1: The goal of this experiment is to test whether the Emotiv EPOC is capable of detecting a P300 peak by co-acting it with P300 Spelling, a program that allows a user to spell words using a cognitive function (recognition). The intended outcome of the experiment is to learn about the P300 peak and to be able to adjust the parameters to achieve the best possible results when analyzing the signals using common EEG signal analysis tools such as EEGLAB, ERPLAB, and BCI2000.

We developed a C# program that imitates how a P300 Speller works and connected it to *testbench*, a tool that captures the EEG signals. The program shows flashing images of numbers 1, 2, 3 and 4, and each time an image flashes, a marker is sent to the Emotiv EPOC recording program. Each image lasts for 1 second, and the next image follows with no delay between images. We used the Com2Com program that virtualizes serial com ports in order to send markers to the *testbench*, as the *testbench* only accepts com ports. After importing the EEG signals to EEGLAB and ERPLAB and inspecting averaged EEG signals per electrode for each possible number for the time frame 0–700 *ms* starting from when the marker was sent and the image was presented, we noticed that only images that corresponded to the answer in mind showed a positive peak in the 300 *ms* time frame after a maker was sent. Participants were asked, "How many years is the fulltime MSc in computer science program?", and only number 2 showed the P300 peak. This initial experiment was conducted on 10 participants, and it indicates that Emotiv EPOC is capable of detecting P300 peaks and is valid for P300 spelling. Subsequently, we used the Emotiv EPOC with BCI2000 using the P300 Speller script, and we were able to spell words by paying attention to the letters that flash on the screen one after the other until words started to form proving the ability of Emotiv EPOC of detecting the P300 peak.

Experiment 0.2: Following Experiment 0.1, we decided to go a step further and test whether it is possible to detect an intention of movement direction. We used the C# program that was used in experiment 0.1, but instead of numbers, we showed images and text of directions ("right" and "left"). We also added the question "In which direction do you intend to go?" in order to place a person who is using the system in the proper context. Five participants participated in this experiment. Each participant read the question and was instructed to look at a monitor that shows possible intended directions. After the images had stopped flashing, we analyzed the recorded EEG signals using EEGLAB and ERPLAB, and the direction that showed a P300 peak was selected as the intended direction of movement. We found that the direction a participant took after viewing the images is exactly the same direction that was detected. Figure 4-1 shows the P300 scalp map in both the intended direction and in the non-intended direction of movement.

Direction Category (Left)
Intention Recognized

Direction Category (Right)
No Recognition

Subject intends to turn left

Figure 4-1. Initial Experiment 0.2 results.

4.1.2   Preliminary Results

Both experiments demonstrated the possibility of detecting a P300 peak using Emotiv EPOC. Experiment 0.2 specifically indicates the possibility of detection of intention before it is executed. These results indicate a possibility in detecting intentions of trusted users who intend to commit maleficence. The detection of such information could constitute a valid approach for designing an access control system that would reject authorized, trusted, and identified users who intend to cause harm to the organization they work for. The next section, Section 4.2, shows the experimental designs employed to achieve the four objectives of this work.

4.2   Experiments

In this Section, we show the design of two experiments:

1) Experiment 1 to investigate the possibility of detecting an intention and detecting the motivation level related to that intention with a hesitation-based design; in this experiment, subjects do not execute the intention. 2) Experiment 2 that addresses both objectives, but in a real insider threat scenario, in order to provide a real sense of detection of a mimicked insider threat incident with a motivation-based design; in this experiment, subjects execute the intention.

The first experiment, Experiment 1, explores the possibility of intent and motivation detection following the single-blind experimental design, which is when the subject does not know the tested intention categories, but only the experimenter knows. We request participants to have a specific intention that they do not aim to execute, using a hesitation-based study (low motivation), and then to test the possibility of detecting that intention with analysis of the data. The second experiment, Experiment 2, also delivers the possibility of intention and motivation detection, but by following a double-blind experimental design, which is when both the subject does not know what intentions they are tested for and the experimenter does not know what intention a subject has among the tested intentions of access, while applying a method of verifying the real intention of a user in order to match the detected intention with the real intention. Also, Experiment 2 delivers the difference in motivation in a real-life insider threat scenario, compared with the first experiment, since, in Experiment 2, participants choose an intention to execute, which uses intrinsically-based motivation. This indicates higher motivation levels compared with the first experiment, which employs extrinsically-based motivation.

Subsequently, the data from both experiments were used as input into the IBAC system for risk assessment and access decision. The analysis of the first objective, intent detection, in both experiments follows a within-subject analysis, detecting intent among possible intent categories. The analysis of the second objective, motivation detection, in both experiments follows a between-subject analysis, differentiating the motivation level between hesitation-based intention, where intent is not executed, and motivation-based intention, where intent is executed. It is expected that all participants in the first experiment are to have a malicious intention being correctly detected, but with low motivation, resulting in low risk and access being granted. In contrast, in the second experiment, it is expected that a malicious intention will be detected along with the high motivation, causing the risk to be high and access to be rejected. The element that confirms motivation level is the post-access monitoring action that a participant performs. If an intention is executed, then motivation should be detected to be high, since low motivation implies less probability of execution of a detected intention.

Table 2 shows the research questions of Experiments 1 and 2 in relation to Objectives 1 and 2.

Table 2. Experiments 1 and 2 in relation to Objectives 1 and 2.

Experiment \ Addressing	Experiment 1 Single-blind (Hesitation-based) (Request specific intent)	Experiment 2 Double-blind (Motivation-based) (Provide freedom of choice to commit a mal-intent, realistic)	Experiments 1 and 2 Overall analysis
Objective 1 (Intent Detection)	Can intentions be detected when a specific task is requested?	Can intentions be detected when chosen freely?	Can intentions be detected in both conditions?
Objective 2 (Motivation Detection)	Can motivation levels be detected? Are they low or high in comparison with Kleih's	Can motivation levels be detected? Are they low or high in comparison with Kleih's [85]	Can motivation levels be detected in both experiments? Are they similar or

	[85] work?	work?	different?

Since the EEG signal is very noisy due to many factors including artificial bioelectric activity (e.g. eye movement, blinks, and muscle activity), environmental electrical activity, and the EEG activity that is not elicited by stimuli (e.g. alpha waves), it is important to address the signal-to-noise ratio (S/N) before designing or analyzing the EEG signal. Luck [90] recommends an important analysis step that is given in the ERP definition: "ERPs are *signal-averaged* epochs of EEG that are time-locked to the onset of stimulus." The averaging step addresses noise, as noise in few trials is lost to averaging. Luck also recommends a designing step in addressing S/N, the number of trials. Setting a correct number of trials is important in designing an ERP experiment. When averaging is used, the S/N increases, yet the size of the signal remains constant, as averaging removes noise in each single trial. As the number of trials increases, the S/N increases, as well; however, Luck states that "If you are focusing on a large component such as the P3 wave, and you expect your experimental manipulation to change the amplitude or latency by a large proportion, then you will need relatively few trials." He continues, "It is important to realize that the relationship between the number of trials and the signal-to-noise ratio is a negatively accelerated function. To be more precise, if R is the amount of noise on a single trial and N is the number of trials, the size of the noise in

an average of the N trials is equal to $(1/\sqrt{N}) * R$. In other words, the remaining noise in an average decreases as a function of the square root of the number of trials." Luck recommends 30 trials for each condition, as a rule of thumb. As a general rule, "it's always better to try to decrease sources of noise than to increase the number of trials."

The following two experiments were designed by taking into consideration the recommendations of Luck [

90] for designing ERP experiments, the P300-based CIT methodology, and Farwell's work [75].

The following experimental design addresses Objectives 1 and 2 of Experiment 1:

4.2.1 Experiment 1 Design: General Intent and Motivation Detection with an Expectation of Intention Not to Be Executed (Hesitation-based).

Experimental Goal:

This experiment is intended to detect the subject's current thoughts toward a specific resource, to further use that information as an input for the access control mechanism. If a participant is thinking of a future plan, past memory, or any thought related to a specific resource, then the thought is detected when the brain recognizes an image that represents that thought. If a participant is thinking of what they intend to do in relation to that resource, then it is a detection of their intentions. A reaction to stimuli that present a view of the intended action would reveal that intention by showing a P300 brain spike, which reflects recognition of the intended action.

This experiment is intended to detect an extrinsically-based intention, which is an intention we impose on participants to have, among non-target possible intentions that participants do not know exist within the system. This experiment is designed to achieve Objective 1, intention detection, and Objective 2, motivation detection, in a hesitation-based experiment design.

Subjects:

A group of 20 participants, both male and female, aged between 18 - 40 years, participated in the experiment, who were recruited via personal emails and local social network. The participants were ensured that they were capable of participating in the experiment prior to signal acquisition. All electronic devices were put away to ensure that the signals are not affected by external sources, and all subjects participated voluntarily with no compensation.

Procedure:

The context of the experiment is to deny a person access to a resource if he or she has projected specific malicious intentions about the use of that resource. For our experiment, we have chosen the action of access to a physical resource (a specific restricted laboratory room). Only having good intents of access such as to study, help, or organize should result in granting access. Having the malicious intention of burning the lab should result in access denied.

Participants in the experiment were asked to have on their mind the malicious intention of burning a lab while looking at random images that they had never seen before. We then started showing various pictures to the participant, including pictures to represent studying, helping and organizing, and pictures showing the lab being set on fire. We then looked to see whether the burning lab pictures triggered any P300 signal, which would indicate a malicious intention toward that space. A P300 signal that is elicited during the showing of images of a person studying, helping someone in, or organizing the lab indicates good intents of access and results in the access request being granted.

Criteria for Selection of Images:

The selected images were chosen so that each image represents an intention. The selection criterion starts by selecting tested intentions (burn lab, study in lab, organize labs, and help study in lab), and continues by choosing images, which is accomplished by searching the name of an intention (e.g. to burn the lab, to study in the lab, to organize the lab, and to help study in the lab). Once the images were selected, we conducted a survey that we distributed to 10 participants who did not participate in the actual experiment, to write what they thought the intention was supposed to be while looking at the images. Only images that received assessments of 90% agreement and above stating that they represented an intention of burning, studying, organizing or helping were selected for the study. This ensures that images depict the category of intention that they are intended to represent, as well as eliminating the possibility of bias. Image selection could result in better accuracy, especially in the case of a specific intent detection. However, this is subject to experimentation in this area. Images could be abstract, as in the use of "malicious intent" vs. "good intent" texts to detect if an intent is malicious or good; however, using such an approach would not determine the exact category of intent, but only the direction of an intent. Each approach is valid for a specific context of deployment, whether it is a public area access or a highly secure facility access. Experiment data analysis is provided in Chapter 5.

Test Environment:

To measure physiological responses of the participant to various images, Emotiv EPOC, a wireless 14-channel EEG acquisition device, was used at a sampling rate of 128 Hz. We used the channels locations AF3, AF4, F3, F4, F7, F8, FC5, FC6, P7, P8, T7, T8, O1, and O2 following the 10-20 standard of electrode placement. Figure 4-2 depicts the Emotiv EPOC electrode placement by Emotiv, and Figure 4-3 depicts the used Emotiv EPOC device.

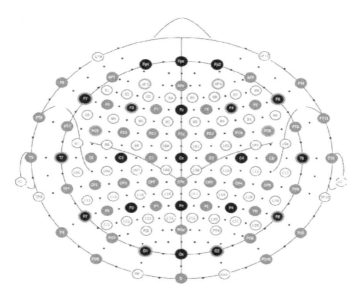

Figure 4-2. Emotiv EPOC electrode placement using the 10-20 placement standard
[91].

Figure 4-3. Emotiv EPOC device.

Participants completed the experiment using a custom system developed to deploy the test and to gather responses from the participants. Participants were first introduced to EPOC before being fitted with this device. The setup was then tested (for approximately 1 minute) to ensure that there was a good signal from the electrodes. EEG data were collected at two times during the experiment: during the baseline and while presenting stimuli. The baseline and reading of stimuli sessions were timed to record precisely for two minutes. Each participant session was recorded as follows:

Following the methodology of P300-based CIT (Section 2.4.3), participants first read the instructions of the experiment that states that they are asked to intend to burn a lab. A sound proof quiet environment was used in order to detect whether our hypothesis was correct or not, without any outside factors that may result in reactions that may mislead the study. However, in future experiments, it should be taken into consideration that the deployment of the access control may not be as quiet as the testing environment. Subsequently, participants were shown their intention in a text statement. This was used to familiarize participants with their intention and to remind them of their intention. Then, the baseline was recorded for one minute. During the baseline phase, participants were asked to relax and were shown a black screen. It was ensured that there was no reflection on the screen. Subsequently, 64 image-based stimuli flashed: 16 stimuli from a target category, which were images that reflect the user's intention, and 48 stimuli from a non-target category, which were images that reflect the user's possible intentions. In this experiment, image stimuli are random pictures of fire, burning papers, and burning books in the target category, and in the non-target category, images were used of random university labs and students studying. As short intervals between target stimuli produce small P300 components [92], we decided that each image should last for 1 second for a session that lasts for 64 seconds, with no inter-stimulus interval. The pattern of flashed stimuli included 3 images from the non-target category and then 1 image from the target category, where each intent category was shown after the every other intent category had been presented. Figure 4-4 depicts the reason for choosing this pattern, which indicates higher P300 amplitude in less time [93]. High P300 amplitude complements the usage of an access control system that can detect intent of access in less time, but with the strongest possible P300 signal.

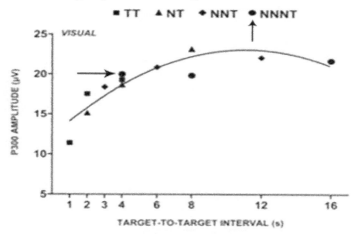

Figure 4-4. Target-to-Target Intervals (TTIs) and the corresponding P300 amplitude
[93].

Each stimulus was used only one time during the session. Target/Non-Target-based markers were automatically sent to *testbench*, the Emotiv EPOC EEG recording system, for analysis. Event markers were sent by using the PortWriter program that sends commands from one serial com port to another. The com0com program, as shown in Figure 4-5, was used to create and map two virtual COM ports together. Figure 4-6, depicts the trend of stimulus onset and the corresponding markers, and Figure 4-7 shows a sample of tested intent categories used in the experiment. The experiment was run once for each participant.

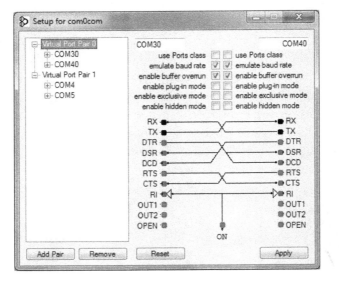

Figure 4-5. The com0com virtual COM port generator.

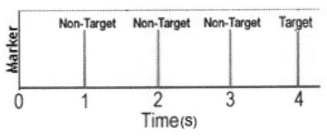

Figure 4-6. Non-Target and Target Markers over time.

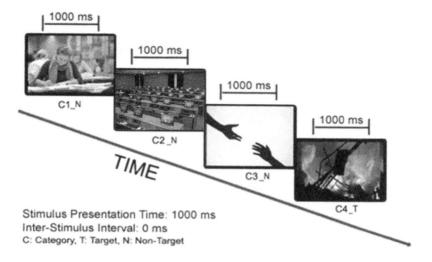

Figure 4-7. Experiment 1 tested Intent Categories.

Since the P300 signal is affected by the brightness of the image and the level of how unexpected an image is among other images, it was anticipated that the fire images might result in a P300 signal regardless of the intent that a participant had. Therefore, a second session of the experiment, a text-based session, was run on all participants that showed white text on a black screen to ensure that the reaction to the category representing an intention is not merely a result of bright images. These image-based vs. text-based experimental sessions compared the effect of using images vs. using text-based stimuli, as well as reporting whether bright images resulted in a P300 signal, or whether the P300 peak rather resulted from a recognition of intent.

4.2.2 Experiment 2 Design: Mimicking an Insider Threat of Viewing High-Level Secure Files with an Expectation of intention being executed (Motivation-based).

Experimental Goal:

The aim of Experiment 2 was to investigate the possibility of insider threat detection using Intent-based Access Control (IBAC). The methodology we apply is intended to detect the existence of an intention to abuse privileges and to detect the specific resource related to the user's plan to commit maleficence. This experiment aimed to detect an intrinsically-based intention, which is an intention that participants choose to have, among possible known intentions, without telling the participants what intention to have and without informing us of what intention they have. This experiment was designed to achieve Objective 1, intention detection, and Objective 2, motivation detection, using a motivation-based experimental design.

Subjects:

A group of 10 university students, both male and female, and aged between 18 - 35 years, participated in the experiment, and were ensured that they were capable of participating in the experiment prior to signal acquisition. All electronic devices were put away to ensure that the experimental signals were not affected by external sources, and all subjects participated voluntarily with no compensation.

Procedure:

Each participant was informed that an important email was sent to all students by the academic advisor to streamline the registration of courses for the next semester. The academic advisors requested students to update their information as soon as possible, and the students were informed that in an hour the system would stop accepting any responses, which would result in problems in their registration. Participants were told that this would require a wired access to the network for them to be able to update their information, and that we were willing to provide them access using our personal laptop only if they did not access a folder named "Personal." The participants were informed that the Personal folder contains private pictures, bank username and password information, critical governmental information, and a diary. Participants were told not to access any of the files unless they could do without getting caught. If they agreed, we then provided them with the laptop to update their information. If they were caught accessing the private information, we informed them that we would end the experiment, as they had failed to open the files without our knowledge. Participants were told not to tell us which file they had opened even after the experiment was complete. Once the participants agreed, we started the experiment. The experimental flow and methodology followed that described for Experiment 1 of showing images that represent four possible intentions: opening the private pictures folder, the bank username and password folder, the critical governmental information folder, or the diary folder. Then participants were able to update their information on a webpage that was already open on the browser and get a period of 2 minutes to open the Personal folder and access one of the files. If there was no recognition of any of the categories of intention, only then access can be legitimate. Figure 4-8 shows a sample of the tested intents categories used in the experiment.

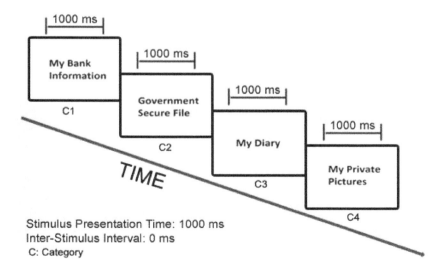

Figure 4-8. Experiment 2 tested Intent Categories.

Criteria for Selection of Images:

The criteria for image selection followed the method of Experiment 1 of selection by surveying 10 students to comment on what each potential image represents.

Procedure Discussion:

Participants were placed in a scenario in which they could be granted legitimate access to a computer. This setup simulates a real-life scenario of an employee gaining access to a data repository. By asking the participants not to open the Personal folder, we simulated a forbidden activity, even though they were able to perform this action. This serves as the abuse of privilege we encounter in insider threats. By stating which files exist in the Personal folder, we provided participants with details of what they could do and to what files. This also simulates a real insider threat scenario, as insiders are aware of the valuable information in an organization. Finally, we informed participants that if they open one of the private files and get caught, we will stop the experiment and they will fail to commit the maleficence without getting caught. We simulate specific acts that an employee is informed not to perform while signing their employment contract and what consequences they may encounter if they are guilty of such a breach.

Since each participant opened a certain file and in order to know what file a participant has opened, if they opened any, we used HyperCam [94], which records the participant's actions while using the laptop. The main reason for asking participants not to report the file they plan to open or have opened is to address the psychological aspect of committing a wrongful act; they need to hide this action, which simulates a real-world scenario. We use the monitor recorder to investigate whether an abuse of privileges occurred or not and to assess the IBAC system to determine if it would have been able to prevent the insider threat. The recordings provide us information that we can use to verify the accuracy of the IBAC system.

Test Environment:

The test environment for Experiment 2 is similar to that of Experiment 1; however, in this experiment, there are no target and non-target intents categories since we do not know what the target intent is. Therefore, each intent category is analyzed separately by looking for a P300 peak to report on detected intention of access. Data analysis is presented in Chapter 5.

CHAPTER 5. Data Analysis, Results and Discussion

5.1 Overview

In this chapter, the two experiments, Experiment 1 and Experiment 2, are analyzed and the results are provided and discussed. The possibility of intention detection using P300 (**Objective 1**) and the detection accuracy using various classification algorithms are provided. Also, the possibility of motivation level detection using the P300 amplitude (**Objective 2**) is addressed. In order to assess the risk of access using Intent-based Access Control (IBAC) (**Objective 3**), the experimental data are analyzed as described by the IBAC's risk assessment component, which was introduced in Section 3.3.3. Subsequently, the results are provided and the potential of IBAC for preventing insider threats is discussed (**Objective 4**). The next sections present the details of the data analysis and results, as well as providing a discussion of the findings.

5.2 Data Analysis and Results

5.2.1 P300 as an Intention Detection Measure (Objective 1)

To detect the P300 signal, we used EEGLAB [95], which is a MATLAB-based EEG signal processing tool that is used for signal pre-processing. EEGLAB provides researchers with various EEG analysis techniques including signal pre-processing, processing, and post-processing. We rely on the capability of EEGLAB in the pre-processing phase only. For processing the EEG signals, we used ERPLAB [98]. ERPLAB provides researchers with various ERP signal extraction techniques. The ERPLAB tool runs on

84

top of EEGLAB and is used for P300 detection, as the P300 is a type of *event-related potential* (ERP). The next two sections show pre-processing and processing of the EEG signals using EEGLAB and ERPLAB, respectively. We then used WEKA to generate and train a classifier model to detect the accuracy of detecting the P300 signal, which was then used to detect intentions of access.

5.2.1.1 Data Pre-Processing Using EEGLAB

The signal pre-processing steps are depicted in Figure 5-1. First, raw EEG data were exported from *testbench* and converted from the European Data Format (EDF) to raw CSV files. For the P300 analysis, only the 14 electrodes' data and the event marker data were selected and imported with a 128 Hz data sampling rate into the EEGLAB tool for pre-processing.

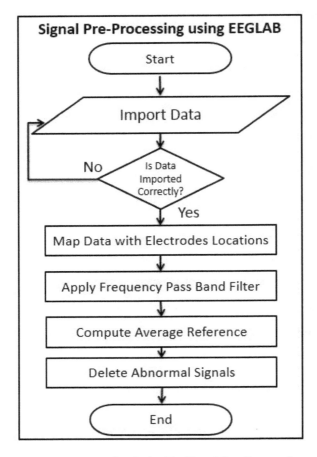

Figure 5-1. Data Analysis (1): Signal Pre-Processing.

Electrode locations were then mapped to the electrode data by importing the emotiv.ced file, which contains the details of each electrode location. Since multiple electrode caps with different electrode channels exist, the electrode location mapping is an important step before analyzing the data and plotting scalp maps. For example, the af3 electrode location information is shown in Figure 5-2. Figure 5-3 shows the channels and their mapped locations, which follows the Emotiv EPOC headset's electrode locations.

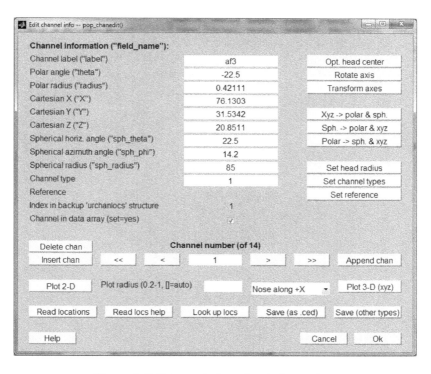

Figure 5-2. Electrode location information.

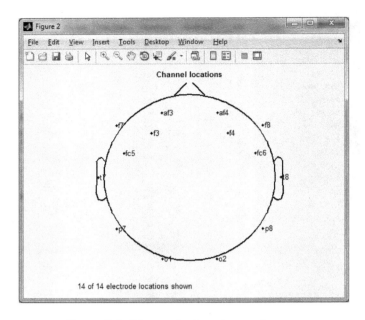

Figure 5-3. Electrodes location scalp map.

Data were then filtered using an FIR filter to identify the delta (1 − 3 Hz) theta (4 - 7 Hz), alpha (8 - 12 Hz), and beta (12 - 20 Hz) bands. Low and high edges of the frequency passband were selected to be 1 Hz and 20 Hz, respectively, to select only the frequency range in which the P300 signal occurs. Figure 5-4 depicts the frequency response when the FIR filter is applied.

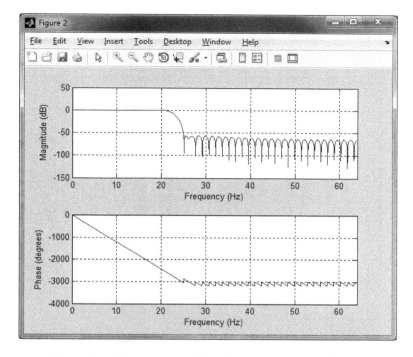

Figure 5-4. Higher edge of the frequency passband (Hz).

Afterwards, the average reference was computed. When electrodes detect electrical signals from the scalp, they measure the difference between one electrode and another, named the reference electrode. In order to avoid a huge difference between electrodes and references, we calculated the average reference and applied it to all instances. "The advantage of average reference rests on the fact that outward positive and negative currents, summed across an entire (electrically isolated) sphere, will sum to 0 (by Ohm's law)" [96].

Finally, data were checked for abnormality and noise using various methods including checking by eye, to detect events such as huge spikes. Any abnormal data were highlighted and rejected from the dataset. Figure 5-5 shows marked and rejected noise in the signals that were identified by human judgment. Further noise rejection was performed in the processing phase using ERPLAB, which is described in Section 5.2.1.2.

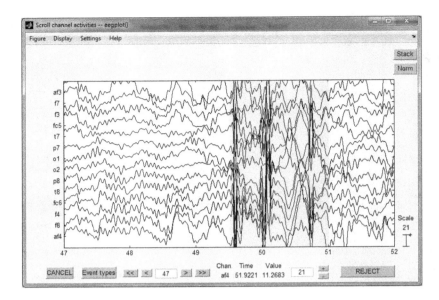

Figure 5-5. Marked and rejected signals.

After pre-processing the data, ERP data were extracted and analyzed as part of the signal processing. The next section, Section 5.2.1.2, Data Processing with ERPLAB, show the ERP plugin that can be used with EEGLAB for the ERP processing. Next, Section 5.2.1.3, Data Classification using WEKA [97], provides the model creation and classification, as well as the ERP detection accuracy. The results are presented in Section 5.2.1.4, and the main findings are described in Section 5.2.1.5.

5.2.1.2   Data Processing Using ERPLAB

Data were processed using the ERPLAB [98] plug-in, which is an analysis tool for ERP data that works on top of EEGLAB. Figure 5-6 depicts the signal processing steps.

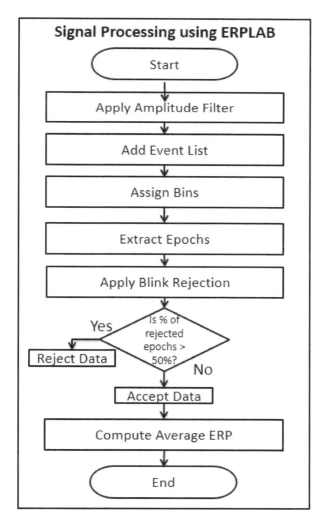

Figure 5-6. Data Analysis (2): Signal Processing.

First, a 0 to 80 µV amplitude filter was applied on continuous data to remove any high amplitude signals within a 500 *ms* sliding window and a 250 *ms* window step on all 14 channels as a noise rejection step. We rejected the data that had over 80 µV value, since electrooculography (EOG), which are the electrical signals that result from blinking and eye movement, artifacts result in 80+ µV. Figure 5-7 shows the marked signals to be rejected due to amplitude.

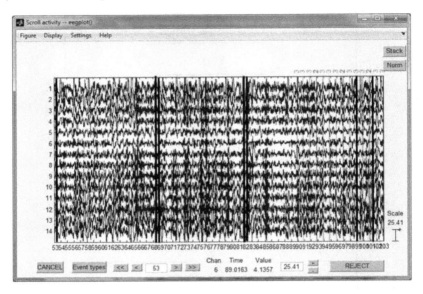

Figure 5-7. Marked signals to be rejected due to noise.

Subsequently, an event list was created to assign each marker (bin) a distinctive label for event-based epoch extraction. We created an event list from ERPLAB by recording the event code number that corresponded to an intent category and its event label such as "Burn Lab, Study" in Experiment 1 and "Accessing Private Pictures, Bank Information" in Experiment 2. Then we added bin numbers starting from number 1. Figure 5-8 shows the event codes.

Currently edited eventcodes			
2	"BurnLab"	1	"1"
3	"Study"	2	"2"
new line			

Figure 5-8. Edited event codes for epoch extraction.

Data epochs were then extracted based on the epoch type (bin number), target stimuli events, and non-target stimuli events, with -100 *ms* to 700 *ms* epoch time, as a P300 peak occurs between 250-500 *ms* after recognition of a stimulus.

Furthermore, artifact detection was used in each epoch to detect eye blinks. If any blink occurred within an epoch, the epoch was deleted. Also, if more than 50% of the epochs were deleted, we discarded the participant data for that intent case. Only 12% or less of the data was rejected across all participants in both experiments. Figure 5-9 shows the epochs rejected by the blink detection method.

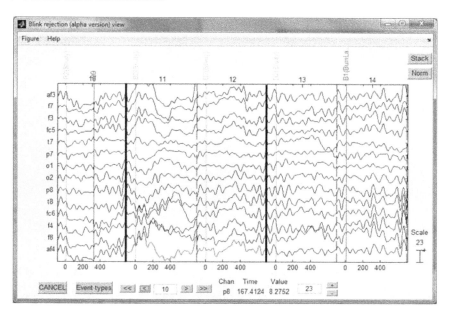

Figure 5-9. Epochs rejected by the blink detection method.

Finally, we computed the average ERPs and plotted each participant's scalp map in all intent categories. The electrode that was closest to the ERP was then selected, and the waveforms in all categories of stimuli were plotted. The closest electrodes for all participants were found to be either of F3, F4, P7, P8, FC5 and FC6.

The event category that shows the P300 peak was then chosen to correspond to the intended action. A sample of the detected P300 peak is the waveform that corresponds to the scalp map and time of activity in between the frontal and partial lobes, as depicted in Figure 5-10.

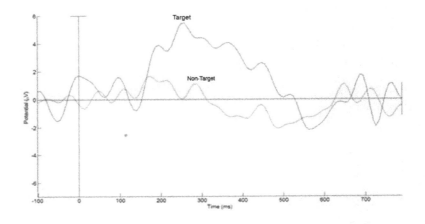

Figure 5-10. P300-based event-related potential (ERP).

5.2.1.2.1   Data Processing Results

After analyzing the data, pre-processing it using EEGLAB, and then processing it using ERPLAB on both experiments, we achieved the results reported in Table 3. Table 3 shows the scalp map with a P300 reaction and the corresponding tested intent category on the left side, along with the P300 amplitude, which is considered as the motivation level. This table also shows the scalp map with no reaction and the corresponding tested intention category on the right side for both experiments. The scalp map

94

with a P300 reaction indicates the user's intent, and the scalp map with no reaction shows the user's unintended action.

Table 3. Scalp map with brain reaction in detected intent category and non-detected intent category in the experiments.

Experiment 1					
P#	**Intent Category Detected To Exist**			**Intent Categories Not Detected To Exist**	
	Scalp Map	Amp	Intent Category	Scalp Map	Intent Category
1		2.9	Burn Lab		Study/Organize Lab/Help
2		2.3	Burn Lab		Study/Organize Lab/Help
3		2.5	Burn Lab		Study/Organize Lab/Help
Experiment 2					
P#	**Intent Category Detected To Exist**			**Intent Categories Not Detected To Exist**	
	Scalp Map	Amp	Intent Category	Scalp Map	Intent Category
1		6.6	Private Pictures		Bank Information, Diary, Government Secure Files

2		6.0	Bank Informa tion		Private Pictures, Diary, Government Secure Files
3		6.5	Govern ment Secure Files		Private Pictures, Diary, Bank Information

Since all participants in Experiment 1 showed a P300 waveform with the "Burn Lab" category, and participants in Experiment 2 showed a P300 waveform with the file they opened, we conclude that P300 shows promise in detecting intentions of access. Figure 5-11 depicts a sample of a participant's reaction to stimuli in the categories Target vs. Non-Target, and Figure 5-12 depicts the P300 waveform in target trials.

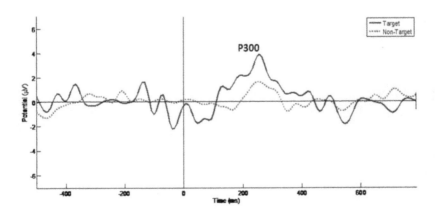

Figure 5-11. Comparison of P300 waveform of F3 for Target and Non-Target Stimuli.

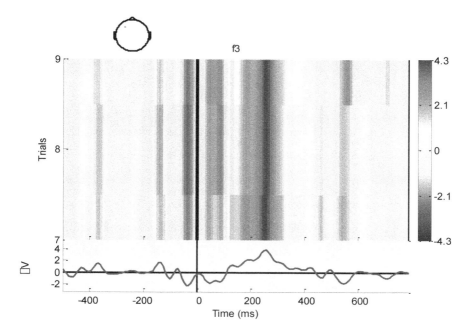

Figure 5-12. P300 waveform of F3 for target trials.

In this section, we explored and identified the future perspective, as opposed to Farwell's work [75, 76] in detecting the past. Intention detection is an underlying principle for the detection of the reason of access. Therefore, we propose the detection of intention information residing in the brain. Unlike Farwell, our approach does not uncover information of a criminal past incident using Guilty Knowledge (GK), but rather prevents an incident from happening by detecting a future intention residing in the brain when using an access control system. Figure 5-13 illustrates the knowledge exploitation module that we propose in order to detect future intentions.

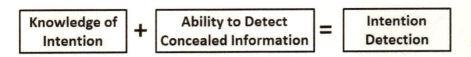

Figure 5-13. Knowledge Exploitation Module.

As the P300 peak shows promise in the detection of the intent category a participant has, we took a further step in differentiating intent categories statistically. If a statistical difference between the intent categories exists, we train classifiers and generate a model that can classify detected and non-detected categories of intentions and report the associated accuracy. The next section presents the statistical analysis as well as the classifier model generation.

5.2.1.3   Data Classification Using WEKA

Waikato environment for Knowledge Analysis (WEKA) is a machine learning platform providing researchers with a set of algorithms in a single program for data mining tasks. The objective of using WEKA is to create and train a classification model to classify the P300 signal from the averaged ERP datasets. The classifier model is then used to classify intentions of access to the tested intention categories. Figure 5-14 depicts the signal classification steps.

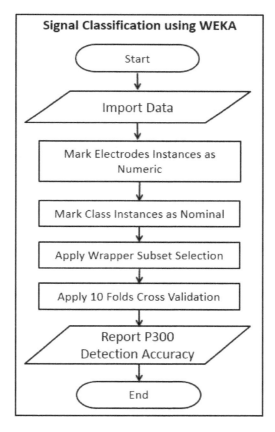

Figure 5-14. Data Analysis (3): Signal Classification.

First, participants' data were exported from ERPLAB to text files for each averaged ERP intent category for each electrode. Then, data for all participants in each category were imported into WEKA to classify each category of intention.

When importing the averaged ERP from ERPLAB into WEKA, a number of features, which describe measurable heuristic properties of the data, were required to be included. Determining a specific collection of features is a key to successful classification. Therefore, we used and compared three sets of features for the model creation. In Set 1, the electrodes for each participant were used as features for the 0–700 ms averaged ERP data set. In Set 2, the features of Set 1 were used, but with a time frame of 200 ms – 500 ms, as the P300-based ERP spike normally resides in this time frame. In Set 3, the features that were used were the maximum value, minimum value, average value, and the standard deviation for each electrode for each participant's ERP dataset. The instances in Set 3 are the maximum, minimum, average and standard deviation of the averaged ERP dataset.

In the three cases, all instances were marked as numeric except for the class type, which was designated as nominal. Then, a supervised attribute selector for best attributes was chosen. For this purpose, we used *wrapper* subset selector for five data mining algorithms (Nearest-Neighbor Classifier, Support Vector Machine (SVM), Random Forest, Neural Networks, and Naïve Bayes). The *wrapper* subset selector tests various combinations of features and reporting the best set of features in order to achieve highest possible accuracy for any given classifier.

In this section, we report the best selected features, based on the accuracy, the sensitivity, the specificity, the False Matching Rate (FMR), and the False Non-Matching Rate (FNMR) of each feature set.

In order to visualize the algorithm's performance, we use the confusion matrix that includes the True Positive, False Positive, True Negative, and False Negative categories. In the context of this book:

True Positive: A user has a **malicious intention** of access and the algorithm detects a **malicious intention**. As a result, the detection of a malicious intention is correct. In this case, access is **denied correctly**, and systems resources have been secured from an insider with a malicious intention. In true positive cases, a correct alert is generated. A malicious insider is detected and denied access.

True Negative: A user has a **good intention** of access and the algorithm detects a **good intention**. As a result, the detection of a good intention is correct. In this case, access is **granted correctly** and no insider threat is detected. In true negative cases, there is a correct absence of alert, and a good insider is granted access.

False Positive: A user has a **good intention** of access and the algorithm detects a **malicious intention**. As a result, the detection of a malicious intention is wrong. In this case, access is **denied incorrectly** and a good insider is denied access. In false positive cases, a false alert is generated, and a good insider is denied access. The false positive rate is also known as the False Matching Rate (FMR).

False Negative: A user has a **malicious intention** of access and the algorithm detects a **good intention**. As a result, the detection of a good intention is wrong. In this case, access is **granted incorrectly** and systems resources are susceptible to an insider threat. In false negative cases, there is a false absence of alert. A malicious insider is not detected, and access is granted. False negative cases are what organizations face daily without insider threat detection techniques. The false negative rate is also known as the False Non-Match Rate (FNMR).

The accuracy measurement is the number of correctly classified instances divided by the total number of tested instances,

$$\frac{\sum Correctly\ Classified\ Instances}{\sum Instances} * 100$$

Sensitivity is a representation of how sensitive the algorithm is, assuring low false negatives and high true positives. Specificity is a representation of how selective the algorithm is in assuring low false positives and high true negatives. Figure 5-15, Figure 5-16 and Figure 5-17 show low sensitivity to high specificity, high sensitivity to low specificity, and high sensitivity to high specificity, and the corresponding false negative rates and false positive rates, respectively.

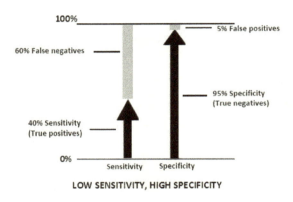

Figure 5-15. Low sensitivity and high specificity

[99]

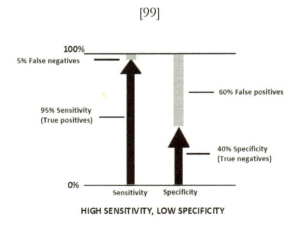

Figure 5-16. High sensitivity and low specificity

[99]

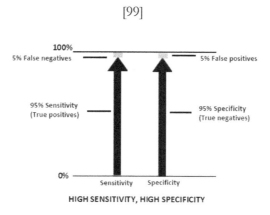

Figure 5-17. High sensitivity and high specificity

[99]

The sensitivity is calculated as $\dfrac{True\ Positive}{(True\ Positive + False\ Negative)} * 100$, and the

specificity is calculated as $\dfrac{True\ Negative}{(True\ Negative + False\ Positive)} * 100$.

As the sensitivity level becomes high, the false negative rate becomes low, but the false positive rate becomes high. Similarly, as the specificity level becomes high, the false positive rate becomes low, but the false negative rate becomes high. Depending on the application, the sensitivity and the specificity levels must be carefully selected.

If the false positive rate needs to be low, so that fewer legitimate users are denied access, the specificity levels are preferred to be higher than the sensitivity levels. In this case, less legitimate users are denied access by accusing them incorrectly of having malicious intentions. This is important, as accusing legitimate users incorrectly is not preferred; however, more malicious insiders will be granted access as the false negative rate will be high.

If the false negative rate needs to be low, so that fewer malicious insiders are granted access, the sensitivity levels are preferred to be higher than the specificity levels. In this case, fewer malicious insiders are granted access. This is very important, as denying malicious insiders may protect an organization from massive destruction; however, more legitimate users are denied access by accusing them incorrectly of having malicious intentions, as false positive rates will be high.

In the case of insider threats, high false negative rates, but with low false positive rates (high specificity) match the reality in which we live: malicious insiders go undetected, but this also indicates that a system is ineffective. On the other hand, high false positive rates, but with low false negative rates (high sensitivity), provide an insider threat detection system, but with many legitimate users being accused of having malicious intentions of access.

The high specificity is no different than the reality in which we live; the insider threat exists with its unbearable risk, but with high sensitivity; the insider threat vanishes, but more legitimate users are accused of what they do not have, a malicious intention.

Normally, an Equal Error Rate (EER) is chosen to find a balance between FMR and FNMR; however, in the case of insider threats, FNMR is very important to be kept very low, to achieve better sensitivity.

If the false negative rate needs to be low, so that fewer malicious insiders are granted access, the sensitivity levels are preferred to be higher than the specificity levels.

The reason we specify the FMR and FNMR instead of the False Acceptance (FAR) and False Rejection Rate (FRR) is that Objectives 1 and 2 are biometric matcher measurements, while Objective 3 is a biometric application measurement. According to Bolle et al. [100], there is difference between a biometric matcher and a biometric application. The intention detection and the motivation level detection are biometric matchers. The IBAC system assessment (Objective 3) is a biometric application. Following are the details describing a biometric matcher and a biometric application:

Biometric   Matcher:

False Match (FM): When two biometric measurements are found to be related to the same intention category, but actually coming from different intention categories, the frequency with which this error occurs is called the False Match Rate (FMR):

$$FMR = \frac{False\ Positive}{(True\ Negative + False\ Positive)} * 100$$

False Non-Match (FNM): When two biometric data measurements are found not to be related to the same intention category, but actually are from the same intention category, the frequency with which this error occurs is called the False Non-Match Rate (FNMR):

$$FNMR = \frac{False\ Negative}{(True\ Positive + False\ Negative)} * 100$$

Biometric Application:

False Accept (FA): When a system decides to grant a user access as a legitimate user while he or she is an imposter, the frequency with which this error occurs is called the False Acceptance Rate (FAR):

$$FAR = \frac{\Sigma\ Number\ False\ Acceptances}{\Sigma\ Number\ of\ Attempts} * 100$$

False Reject (FR): When a system decides to deny a user access as an imposter while he or she is a legitimate user, the frequency with which this error occurs is called the False Rejection Rate (FRR):

$$FRR = \frac{\sum Number\ of\ False\ Rejections}{\sum Number\ of\ Attempts} * 100$$

Table 4 indicates the accuracy, sensitivity, specificity, False Match Rate, and False Non-Match Rate, which metrics will be used to report the algorithm performance for all tested algorithms presented in this book.

Table 4. Accuracy, sensitivity, specificity, FMR and FNMR.

Measurement	Value
Accuracy	$\frac{\sum Correctly\ Classified\ Instances}{\sum Instances} * 100$
Sensitivity	$\frac{True\ Positive}{(True\ Positive + False\ Negative)} * 100$
Specificity	$\frac{True\ Negative}{(True\ Negative + False\ Positive)} * 100$
False Match Rate (FMR) (Type 1 Error)	$\frac{False\ Positive}{(True\ Negative + False\ Positive)} * 100$
False Non-Match Rate (FNMR) (Type 2 Error)	$\frac{False\ Negative}{(True\ Positive + False\ Negative)} * 100$

5.2.1.4   Results

Using Feature Set 1, statistics suggest that the target vs. non-target intent categories are different from one another. A two-tailed t test uncovers that for the intent category in the ERP waveform when viewing intention category-related stimuli, compared with non-intent category-related stimuli ($p \leq .005$ as seen in Table 5). Table 5 all features except for O2 show a statistically significant difference between the two classes. Only those features were used to train a classifier to differentiate between the classes of intention.

Table 5. *t*-test for EEG signals in Set 1 of features.

Two-Tailed Paired Samples T-Test					
Feature	Target Stimuli		Non-Target Stimuli		P value
	Mean	STD	Mean	STD	
AF3	0.650621	4.011416	-0.54195	2.77626	1.22E-27
F7	0.441488	4.056893	-0.18965	2.557644	5.31E-12
F3	-0.36546	3.383893	0.352824	1.717832	2.01E-17
FC5	0.240313	2.967626	-0.08775	1.630703	2.04E-06
T7	0.627111	3.7039	-0.08366	1.8681	5.31E-14
P7	-0.28513	3.447893	-0.0001	1.809565	0.000713
O1	-0.43862	3.87856	-0.13918	1.892136	0.000902
O2	**-0.14167**	**4.387815**	**-0.07455**	**2.224363**	**0.482974**
P8	-0.05207	3.386018	0.273787	1.821748	7.61E-05
T8	-0.67635	3.628576	0.36694	1.994857	2.83E-26
FC6	-0.36209	2.849143	0.044582	1.552893	6.91E-08
F4	-0.04388	3.514306	0.305885	1.677481	6.91E-05
F8	-0.26114	4.406859	0.082364	2.641675	0.001506
AF4	0.666862	4.054723	-0.30954	2.387751	8.88E-19

By comparing the signal deviation between the classes of intention, we notice that target stimuli show higher deviation values compared with non-target stimuli, which indicates a signal change in the target signals compared with non-target signals. Figure 5-18 shows the deviation.

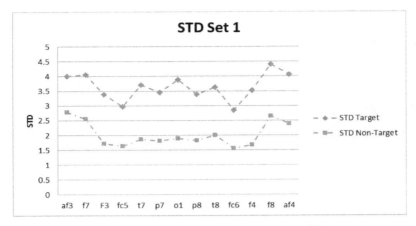

Figure 5-18. Standard deviations of Set 1 of features

In Feature Set 2, statistics suggest that target vs. non-target intent categories are different from one another. A two-tailed t test uncovers that for the intent category in the ERP waveform when viewing intention category-related stimuli, compared with non-intent category-related stimuli ($p \leq .05$ as seen in Table 6).

Table 6 shows all features except for $F8$ and $O2$ show statistically significant differences between the two classes. All features except $F8$ and $O2$ were used to train a classifier to differentiate between the classes of intention.

Table 6. *t*-test for EEG signals in Set 2 of features.

Two-Tailed Paired Samples T-Test					
Feature	Target Stimuli		Non-Target Stimuli		P value
	Mean	STD	Mean	STD	
AF3	0.809129	4.225099	-0.65557	2.98933	1.08E-15
F7	0.634337	4.600938	-0.37916	2.921047	1.93E-10
F3	-0.81813	3.660913	0.493168	1.765868	2.87E-22
FC5	0.497342	3.297253	-0.14117	1.817545	8.16E-08
T7	0.679297	3.744582	-0.13189	2.115932	6.63E-08
P7	-0.11869	3.868955	0.208766	1.803941	0.022447
O1	-0.42424	4.415021	-0.0681	1.824912	0.027345
O2	**-0.11622**	**4.764677**	**0.060299**	**2.470093**	**0.263054**
P8	0.083159	3.570381	0.381089	1.971294	0.028904
T8	-0.77012	3.85311	0.331569	2.151914	4.7E-12
FC6	-0.45018	3.217628	0.009929	1.637126	0.000344
F4	-0.34309	3.615241	0.375378	1.766959	1.08E-07
F8	**-0.14443**	**4.378101**	**-0.03492**	**2.810058**	**0.53072**
AF4	0.48182	4.315791	-0.44939	2.664195	9.63E-07

By comparing the signal deviation between the classes of intention, we notice that target stimuli show higher deviation compared with non-target stimuli, which indicates a signal change in the target signals compared with non-target signals. Figure 5-19 shows the deviation.

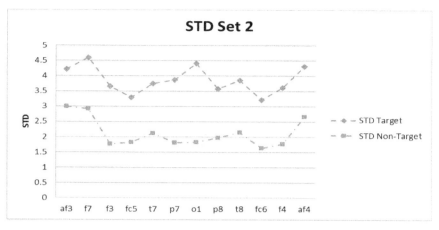

Figure 5-19. Standard deviations of Set 2 of features

In Feature Set 3, statistics suggest that target vs. non-target intent categories are different from one another. A two-tailed t-test shows that the intent category in the ERP waveform when viewing intention category-related stimuli, compared with non-intent category-related stimuli ($p \leq 0.05$ as seen in Table 7).

Table 7 all features except for AF3MIN and all 14 average features (AF3 – AF4) show statistically significant differences between the two classes. Only those features were used to train a classifier to differentiate between the classes of intention.

Table 7. *t*-test for EEG signals in Set 3 of features.

Two-Tailed Paired Samples T-Test					
Feature	Target Stimuli		Non-Target Stimuli		P value
	Mean	STD	Mean	STD	
AF3MAX	7.204952	3.332408	3.191294	1.390299	0.000104
F7MAX	6.717554	2.993456	3.703405	1.431664	0.000122
F3MAX	5.602177	2.830957	3.14735	1.321553	0.000426
FC5MAX	5.35621	2.493862	2.717832	1.127218	0.000143
T7MAX	6.848787	5.202875	3.385123	1.544569	0.00696
P7MAX	5.527473	2.70705	3.313926	1.611992	0.00086
O1MAX	5.824973	3.315588	3.378415	1.860487	0.002667
O2MAX	6.940293	4.782075	4.045051	2.85715	0.002701
P8MAX	6.254222	4.402191	3.63111	2.21232	0.009388
T8MAX	5.850436	3.619003	3.334464	2.361067	0.002201
FC6MAX	4.396876	1.810235	2.755692	1.683214	0.000518
F4MAX	5.237806	2.846231	3.07138	1.243162	0.001304
F8MAX	7.014712	4.029736	4.027938	2.424824	0.001818
AF4MAX	7.612029	3.856165	3.40502	1.349341	3.14E-05
AF3MIN	**-5.92409**	**4.056169**	**-4.53445**	**3.370271**	**0.156632**
F7MIN	-5.88704	4.946679	-4.16181	2.933606	0.033563
F3MIN	-6.28978	3.659636	-2.53406	1.775893	5.14E-05
FC5MIN	-4.81894	2.748679	-2.73519	1.651796	0.000983
T7MIN	-5.70042	3.124697	-3.20146	1.465879	0.000701
P7MIN	-6.74761	4.04669	-3.1683	1.652223	0.000961
O1MIN	-6.36455	3.329766	-3.46788	1.665775	0.000961
O2MIN	-7.56682	3.953287	-4.04485	1.813246	0.000168
P8MIN	-6.13032	3.116662	-2.90281	1.1583	2.36E-05
T8MIN	-6.91942	3.99346	-2.68892	0.962131	0.000148

FC6MIN	-4.74477	2.288567	-2.65374	1.232314	0.00222
F4MIN	-4.86179	3.32642	-2.81741	1.5478	0.016864
F8MIN	-7.03241	3.661152	-4.04273	1.854974	0.002391
AF4MIN	-5.99105	2.783016	-3.77883	2.657455	0.021188
AF3AVG	**0.650621**	**2.444151**	**-0.54195**	**2.12561**	**0.109997**
F7AVG	**0.441488**	**2.822144**	**-0.18965**	**1.709641**	**0.221839**
F3AVG	**-0.36546**	**1.955512**	**0.352824**	**1.207744**	**0.155965**
FC5AVG	**0.240313**	**1.800897**	**-0.08775**	**1.056046**	**0.362446**
T7AVG	**0.627111**	**2.047213**	**-0.08366**	**1.206227**	**0.206141**
P7AVG	**-0.28513**	**1.730622**	**-0.0001**	**0.914198**	**0.501478**
O1AVG	**-0.43862**	**2.538061**	**-0.13918**	**0.969892**	**0.596354**
O2AVG	**-0.14167**	**2.618376**	**-0.07455**	**1.310781**	**0.88787**
P8AVG	**-0.05207**	**1.621392**	**0.273787**	**0.958653**	**0.459105**
T8AVG	**-0.67635**	**2.019386**	**0.36694**	**1.436537**	**0.095794**
FC6AVG	**-0.36209**	**1.689758**	**0.044582**	**0.984267**	**0.404772**
F4AVG	**-0.04388**	**2.419404**	**0.305885**	**0.96275**	**0.557901**
F8AVG	**-0.26114**	**2.688784**	**0.082364**	**1.898797**	**0.62703**
AF4AVG	**0.666862**	**2.357569**	**-0.30954**	**1.656919**	**0.199216**
AF3STD	3.032445	1.098735	1.793978	0.820777	7.57E-06
F7STD	2.803178	1.161726	1.881994	0.648193	9.89E-05
F3STD	2.598834	1.108449	1.257343	0.387591	2.41E-06
FC5STD	2.290648	0.76015	1.25464	0.384105	9.23E-07
T7STD	2.809989	1.374931	1.452755	0.423357	4E-05
P7STD	2.784989	1.129555	1.520645	0.50966	5.28E-06
O1STD	2.818411	1.013027	1.574411	0.540184	1.68E-07
O2STD	3.320515	1.444362	1.745371	0.667559	1.95E-06
P8STD	2.74925	1.277466	1.488097	0.624121	1.14E-05
T8STD	2.763837	1.405659	1.403008	0.547977	3.83E-05

FC6STD	2.123252	0.79723	1.194104	0.374917	9.5E-06
F4STD	2.415941	1.042766	1.33287	0.462729	1.62E-06
F8STD	3.238225	1.132111	1.876292	0.65992	7.25E-06
AF4STD	3.093815	1.195197	1.689021	0.679884	6.34E-07

By comparing the signal deviation between the classes of intention, we notice that target stimuli show higher deviations compared with non-target stimuli, which indicates a signal change in the target signals compared with non-target signals. Figure 5-20 shows the deviation.

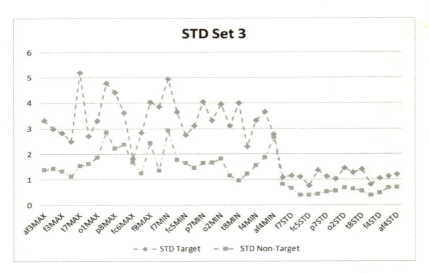

Figure 5-20. Standard deviations of Set 3 of features (af3MAX – af4 STD).

As the statistics suggest a difference between target vs. non-target stimuli in all three sets of features, we investigate and report the ability to detect the category of an intention of access and the intention detection accuracy using WEKA. The details are provided in the next section.

5.2.1.4.1 Intention Detection Accuracy Using WEKA

For Feature Set 1 of the Electrodes Only:

After generating the model with a 10-fold cross-validation test metric for each algorithm, we uncovered the accuracy results shown in Table 8:

Table 8. Feature Set 1 Results.

Classifier	Features	Number of Features	Accuracy Rate
Nearest-Neighbor Classifier	**F7, FC5, T7, P7, O1, P8, T8, FC6, F4 and F8**	**10 features**	**96.55%**
SVM	F7, FC5, T7, P7, O1, P8, T8, FC6, F4 and F8	10 features	95.68%
Random Forest	F7, FC5, T7, O1, P8, T8, FC6, F4 and F8	9 features	91.16%
Neural Networks	F7, FC5, T7, P7, O1, P8, T8, FC6, F4 and F8	10 features	85.97%
Naïve Bayes	F7, FC5, T7, P7, O1, T8, FC6 and F8	8 features	75.62%

The best classifiers for the P300-based intention detection in Set 1 are Nearest Neighbor and Support Victor Machine with 96.55% and 95.68% accuracy, respectively. Then, the classifiers Random Forest, Neural Networks, and Naïve Bayes had reported accuracy values of 91.16%, 85.97%, and 75.62%, respectively.

The Nearest Neighbor classifier reported FNMR, which maps to an insider with malicious intention not being detected by the system, of 0.91% as the lowest measured rate. Other classifiers reported the rates of 1.27% 4.54%,

8.43%, and 13.33% for SVM, Random Forest, Neural Networks, and Naïve Bayes classifiers, respectively. The Nearest Neighbor classifier reported 5.97% FMR, which metric describes an insider with good intent being reported to have a malicious intention, as the best FMR among all classifiers. SVM, Random Forest, Neural Networks, and Naïve Bayes reported 7.35%, 13.13%, 19.62%, and 35.41% FMR values, respectively.

The best set of features is F7, FC5, T7, P7, O1, P8, T8, FC6, F4, and F8, using the Nearest Neighbor classifier, with an accuracy rate of 96.55%.

For Feature Set 2 (Identical to Feature Set 1 but for 200 *ms* – 500 *ms)*

After generating the model with a 10-fold cross-validation test metric for each algorithm, we discovered the accuracy results in Table 9:

Table 9. Feature Set 2 Results.

Classifier	Features	Number of Features	Accuracy Rate
Nearest-Neighbor Classifier	F7, F3, FC5, T7, O1, T8 and F4	7 features	99.35%
SVM	**F7, F3, FC5, T7, P7, O1, P8, T8, FC6, and F4**	**10 features**	**99.59%**
Random Forest	F7, F3, T7, O1, T8, and FC6	6 features	96.25%
Neural Networks	F7, F3, FC5, T7, P7, O1, P8, T8, FC6, and F4	10 features	95.08%
Naïve Bayes	F3, T7, O1 and T8	4 features	80.06%

The best classifiers for the P300-based intention detection in Set 2 are SVM and Nearest Neighbor, with 99.59% and 99.35% accuracy, respectively. Then, the classifiers Random Forest, Neural Networks, and Naïve Bayes reported accuracy values of 96.25%, 95.08%, and 80.06%, respectively.

The SVM classifier reported FNMR, which maps to an insider with malicious intention, not being detected by the system, with its value of 0.58% representing the best rate among all classifiers. Other classifiers reported the rates of 1.05%, 4.56%, 5.61%, and 27.13% for Nearest Neighbor, Random Forest, Neural Networks, and Naïve Bayes classifiers, respectively. The SVM and Nearest Neighbor classifiers reported 0.23% FMR, which describes an insider with good intentions being reported to have malicious intentions, as the best FMR value among all classifiers. Random Forest, Neural Networks, and Naïve Bayes classifiers reported 2.92% 4.21%, and 12.74% FMR values, respectively.

The best set of features is FC5MAX, T8MIN, FC6MIN, F4MIN, F8MIN, FC5STD and FC6STD combined with the classifier SVM, with an accuracy rate of 100%.

For Feature Set 3 (MAX-MIN-AVG-STD for Each Electrode):

After generating the model with a 10-fold cross-validation test metric for each algorithm, we determined the accuracy results in Table 10:

Table 10. Feature Set 3 Results.

Classifier	Features	Number of Features	Accuracy Rate
Nearest-Neighbor Classifier	FC5MAX, T7MAX, P7MAX, F7MAX, T7STD, O1STD and T8STD	4 MAX type and 3 STD type for total 7 features	100%
SVM	FC5MAX, T8MIN, FC6MIN, F4MIN, F8MIN, FC5STD and FC6STD	1 MAX type, 4 MIN type and 2 STD type for total 7 features	100%
Random Forest	**F4MAX, F8MAX, P8MIN, F7STD, F3STD and T7STD**	**2 MAX type, 1 MIN type and 3 STD type for total 6 features**	**100%**

Neural Networks	T8MIN, FC5STD and F4STD	1 MIN type and 2 STD type for 3 features	98.68%
Naïve Bayes	T8MIN, FC5STD and FC6STD	One feature from the 1 MIN type and 2 STD for total 3 features	97.80%

The best classifiers for the P300-based intention detection in Set 3 are Nearest Neighbor, SVM, and Random Forest, each with 100% accuracy. Then, the classifiers Neural Networks and Naïve Bayes had reported accuracy values of 98.68% and 97.80%, respectively.

Nearest Neighbor, SVM, and Random Forest classifiers reported FNMR values, which map to an insider with malicious intention not being detected by the system, of 0%. The Neural Networks and Naïve Bayes classifiers had reported FNMR rates of 2.63% and 3.50%, respectively. Nearly all classifiers reported 0% FMR, representing an insider with good intentions being reported to have malicious intentions, except for Naïve Bayes, which had a reported FMR value of 0.87%.

The best set of features is F4MAX, F8MAX, P8MIN, F7STD, F3STD and T7STD with the classifier Random Forest, with an accuracy rate of 100% and only 6 features.

Feature Set 3 shows standard deviation features to be the best among the other types of features.

Table 11 summarizes Feature Sets 1, 2 and 3 and the classifiers' results of accuracy, sensitivity, specificity, False Match Rates, and False Non-Match Rates. The best algorithms in terms of accuracy are bolded.

Table 11. Accuracy of detecting intentions of access using different classifiers.

Accuracy of P300 as an Intention Measure Using Different Classifiers					
Classifier / Results		N N	S V M	R F	N N e t	N B
Feature Set 1 (Electro des Only)	Accuracy	96.55%	95.68%	91.16%	85.97%	75.62%
	Sensitivity	98.70%	98.63%	95.02%	90.50%	82.89%
	Specificity	93.20%	93.06%	87.90%	82.35%	79.99%
	FMR	0.91%	1.27%	4.54%	8.43%	13.33%
	FNMR	5.97%	7.35%	13.13%	19.62%	35.41%
Feature Set 2 (Set 1, but with 200 ms – 500 ms)	Accuracy	99.35%	99.59%	96.25%	95.08%	80.06%
	Sensitivity	99.76%	99.76%	97.02%	95.72%	85.11%
	Specificity	98.95%	99.41%	95.51%	94.46%	76.27%
	FMR	0.23%	0.23%	2.92%	4.21%	12.74%
	FNMR	1.05%	0.58%	4.56%	5.61%	27.13%
Feature Set 3 (Electro des MAX, MIN, AVG and	Accuracy	100%	100%	100%	98.68%	97.80%
	Sensitivity	100%	100%	100%	100%	99.10%
	Specificity	100%	100%	100%	97.43%	96.58%
	FMR	0	0	0	0	0.87%

STD)	FNMR	0	0	0	2.63%	3.50%

A comparison between Feature Sets 1, 2 and 3 is presented in Figures 5-(21-25), showing the difference in accuracy, sensitivity, specificity, FMR, and FNMR. Clearly, Feature Set 2 achieves better accuracy, sensitivity, specificity, FMR and FNMR results compared with Feature Set 1. Feature Set 3 clearly exhibits the best results in the metrics of accuracy, sensitivity, specificity, FMR, and FNMR with the classifiers Nearest Neighbor, SVM, and Random Forest, compared with Feature Sets 1 and 2. Feature Set 3 achieved the best results when detecting an intention category with the Random Forest classifier, using only the 6 features F4MAX, F8MAX, P8MIN, F7STD, F3STD and T7STD. The second-best performance rank is given to both the Nearest Neighbor classifier with only the 7 features FC5MAX, T7MAX, P7MAX, F7MAX, T7STD, O1STD, and T8STD, and to the SVM classifier with the 7 features FC5MAX, T8MIN, FC6MIN, F4MIN, F8MIN, FC5STD, and FC6STD. Both had an accuracy of 100% as the best accuracy rate.

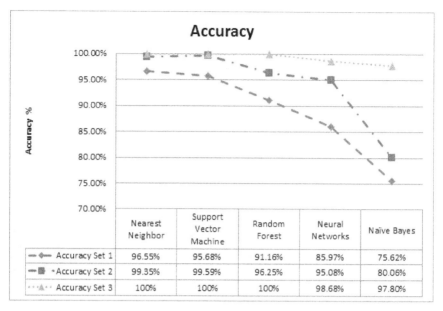

Figure 5-21. Comparison of accuracy between Feature Sets 1, 2 and 3

	Nearest Neighbor	Support Vector Machine	Random Forest	Neural Networks	Naïve Bayes
Accuracy Set 1	96.55%	95.68%	91.16%	85.97%	75.62%
Accuracy Set 2	99.35%	99.59%	96.25%	95.08%	80.06%
Accuracy Set 3	100%	100%	100%	98.68%	97.80%

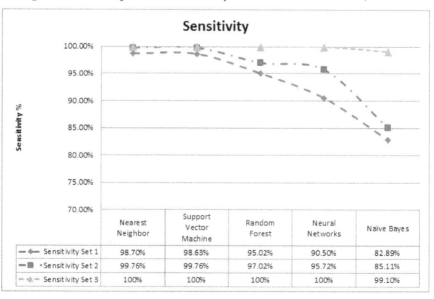

	Nearest Neighbor	Support Vector Machine	Random Forest	Neural Networks	Naïve Bayes
Sensitivity Set 1	98.70%	98.63%	95.02%	90.50%	82.89%
Sensitivity Set 2	99.76%	99.76%	97.02%	95.72%	85.11%
Sensitivity Set 3	100%	100%	100%	100%	99.10%

Figure 5-22. Comparison of sensitivity between Feature Sets 1, 2 and 3.

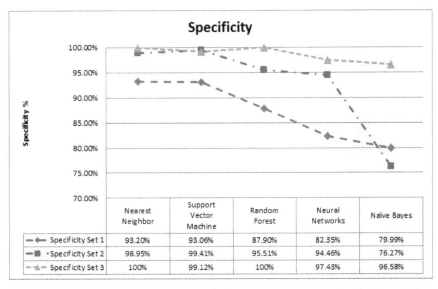

Figure 5-23. Comparison of specificity between Feature Sets 1, 2 and 3.

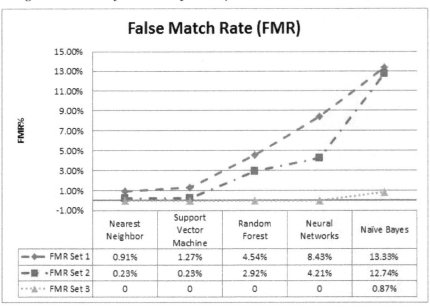

Figure 5-24. Comparison of FMR between Feature Sets 1, 2 and 3.

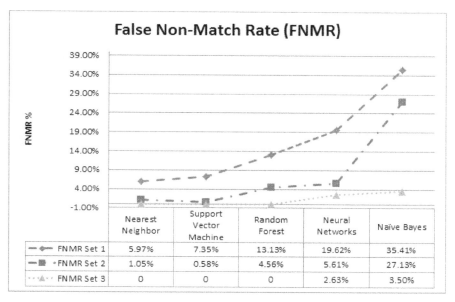

False Non-Match Rate (FNMR)

	Nearest Neighbor	Support Vector Machine	Random Forest	Neural Networks	Naïve Bayes
FNMR Set 1	5.97%	7.35%	13.13%	19.62%	35.41%
FNMR Set 2	1.05%	0.58%	4.56%	5.61%	27.13%
FNMR Set 3	0	0	0	2.63%	3.50%

Figure 5-25. Comparison of FNMR between Feature Sets 1, 2 and 3.

5.2.1.5   Main Findings

By addressing the limitations of brain "fingerprinting" identified in [101, 102], we proposed and discovered a different perspective of brain fingerprinting. First, using the 30 participants' brain reactions to visual stimuli in both experiments, we demonstrated that P300 is a valid measure for intention detection by stimulating the brain by asking about the intention of an action and showing possible intentions. An intention recognition identified by eliciting a P300 peak is evidence of the existence of the intention information residing in the brain, given that everyone knows their intention of an action. In both experiments, having in mind the intention of burning a lab and opening a personal file maliciously, the 30 participants showed P300 peaks only in the "Burning Lab" category in the case of Experiment 1 and in the specific personal file target stimuli in Experiment 2. These results suggest that P300 is a valid approach for identifying what a person is intending by showing him or her an image of the intended thought. The experimental results support the validity of the hypothesis stating the possibility of intention detection by the analysis of the EEG signals of individuals related to the recognition of their intentions using P300 data. The statistics suggest a differentiation of the EEG signals when viewing an intent category that relates to an intention and the intent category that does not relate to an intention. The classification accuracy of 100% using SVM, Nearest Neighbor, and Random Forest classifiers supports the tested hypothesis.

Further, as stated in Section 4.2.1, Experiment 1, the P300 peak may have been elicited as a result of bright and unexpected images of fire compared with studying, organizing lab and helping images. Therefore, a text-based session was run on all participants in order to report whether or not the P300 peak is to be elicited to the same intent category similar to the image-based session.

The analysis of the text-based session was performed similarly to that of the image-based session, and it shows a P300 peak only in the "Burn Lab" intent category among the other categories, which indicates the validity of the method in recognizing an intention similar to the results in Experiment 2, involving the accessing of a restricted folder.

However, the results from the text-based session show lower P300 amplitude compared with the image-based session, with an average difference of 0.098 μV. These findings indicate that bright images may result in higher amplitude in the hesitation-based experiment.

Comparing the hesitation-based experiment with the motivation-based experiment answered the question of the motivation level difference, Objective 2. Comparing the image-based session in Experiment 1 with the text-based experiment of Experiment 2 is considered a worst-case scenario, and if these varied conditions show a clear difference, then comparing the text-based session in Experiment 1 with the text-based experiment in Experiment 2 should also show a clear difference. The next section, Section 5.2.2, presents the investigation of motivation level detection (Objective 2).

5.2.2   P300   Amplitude   as   a   Motivation   Measure (Objective 2)

Because motivation has been reported to influence the P300 signal amplitude by Kelih *et al.* [85], we hypothesize that the signal amplitude is also a determination of motivation level, where the P300 waveform when viewing target stimuli becomes higher than the waveform in the 200 - 500 *ms* window of the corresponding signal when viewing non-target stimuli.

A one-tailed *t-test* reveals the amplitude of the P300 waveform when viewing target stimuli in both experiments (M = 3.90, SD = 1.61) compared with the highest amplitude of a 200 *ms* window of corresponding signal when viewing non-target stimuli in both experiments (M = 1.79, SD = 0.41), p ≤ 0.0005. This indicates a differentiation between the signal amplitude in the target vs. non-target cases, showing higher amplitude in the target stimuli compared with non-target stimuli.

Further, a two-tailed *t*-test shows the amplitude in the P300 waveform when viewing target stimuli in Experiment 1 (M = 2.97, SD = 0.08) compared with the amplitude when viewing target stimuli in Experiment 2 (M = 5.82, SD = 0.06), p ≤ 0.0005. This indicates a differentiation between the signal amplitude in the P300 amplitude in Experiment 1 when viewing target stimuli compared with the P300 amplitude in Experiment 2 when viewing target stimuli. It also indicates that the P300 amplitude is higher in Experiment 2 when viewing target stimuli than the P300 amplitude in Experiment 1 when viewing target stimuli. Given that none of the participants executed their intention in Experiment 1, but all participants executed their intentions in Experiment 2, this indicates that the signal amplitude corresponds to the likelihood of an intent execution.

Moreover, by comparing the results in [85] with a mean of $\mu = 4.89$ with no motivation and $\mu = 6.1$ for high motivation, we find that Experiment 1 shows a mean average of $\mu = 2.97$ of motivation for requesting access to a lab with an intention of burning it, which is less motivation than the reported means in [85] in all categories. This indicates that participants of Experiment 1 had low motivation to execute their intentions. Also, by comparing the results in [85] with Experiment 2, which had an average of $\mu = 5.82$, which resides right below the tested high motivation in [85], we conclude that the participants in Experiment 2 were motivated to execute their intentions.

These findings result in the conclusion that the participants in Experiment 1 recognized their intentions, but were not motivated to execute them, while participants in Experiment 2 recognized their intentions and were motivated to execute them. We conclude that the P300 amplitude can effectively describe how an intention is most likely to happen, which is based on the motivation level that corresponds to a specific intention.

5.2.3   IBAC System Assessment (Objective 3)

IBAC is an access control model that grants or denies access based on the intentions of subjects and the corresponding motivation levels. It is based on the current measurements of the physiological signals that subjects emit involuntarily at the time of access request. The physiological signals allow the determination of the intent of the subject and the motivation level, and hence form a decision about what level of access should be given, if any.

Since IBAC uses physiological signals in order to form a decision about access, it is assessed as a biometric system; however, there exist differences in the objectives of IBAC compared with other biometric systems. The differences lie in the authentication of intents instead of identities when providing access decisions. In contrast to identity-based biometric systems, in IBAC we do not rely on identifying different individual features to distinguish identities, but we rather use similar individual features that determine intents. In IBAC, the intent is always assumed to be malicious unless proven otherwise.

The assessment of the potential of IBAC in detecting and preventing the insider threat requires:

1- The detected intention; 2- The motivation level; 3- The intent category risk; and 4- The asset value.

Although the intention detection and motivation level are determined by the IBAC system, in order to provide an accurate risk level, the intent category risk needs to be determined with high accuracy by the asset owner. Also, in order to provide an accurate estimate of the asset loss in value if access is granted, the asset value needs to be determined by the asset owner, as well, and used as an input to the system. Both intent category risk and asset value can be determined by having an insider threat assessment already in place in the organization where IBAC is deployed as an insider threat control mechanism.

IBAC provides intelligence that was not available in the past for assessing the risk of access and the expected asset loss if access is granted. It is left to the organization that is deploying IBAC to select a threshold value of accepted loss. As in any risk-based control method, the provided intelligence is intended to assess and support a decision of access, rather than to determine an access decision. As stated in the Access Decision component in the IBAC design (Section 3.3.3.1), the decision is determined by the accepted threshold that the organization deploying IBAC has selected, as well as the type of decision that is determined, such as whether access is to be restricted, access levels to be determined, or any other decision sought by the organization.

Based on the results in Sections 5.2.1 (**Objective 1, Intent Detection**) and 5.2.2 (**Objective 2, Motivation Detection**), IBAC is capable of detecting the category of an intention, and the probability that that intention is to be executed with varying degrees of risk, as seen in Figure 5-26 in the image-based experiment session of Experiment 1 and Experiment 2 and Figure 5-27 in the text-based experiment session of Experiment 1 and Experiment 2. The varying degrees of probability of an intention to be executed and the ability to detect an intention provide the risk if access is to be granted. Current access control systems fail to do so, and grant access based on identity. The impact of using images as stimuli shows that at a risk level of 40 as a threshold, the system results in 0% falsely accepted, 95% correctly accepted, 5% falsely rejected and 100% correctly rejected users.

If the risk level is to be set at 46 as a threshold, the system results in 20% falsely accepted, 100% correctly accepted, 0% falsely rejected and 80% correctly rejected users, which means that the new technology does not result in a negative impact in rejecting a legitimate user compared with the risk threshold of 40, but with 80% of insiders being correctly rejected.

When using text as a stimulus, we avoid the impact of bright images on the P300 amplitude. With a risk level of 35 as a threshold, the system results in 0% falsely accepted, 100% correctly accepted, 0% falsely rejected and 100% correctly rejected users, which means that the new technology does not result in a negative impact with 100% of insiders being correctly rejected.

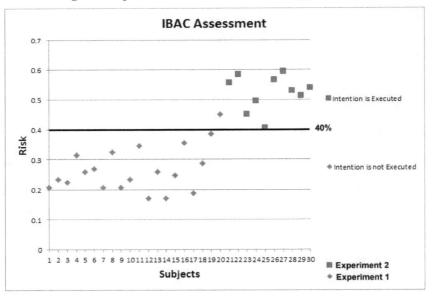

Figure 5-26. Risk level corresponding to the executed vs. non-executed malicious intentions groups (experiments 1:image-based and experiment 2: text-based).

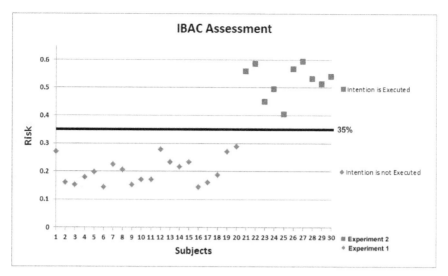

Figure 5-27. Risk level corresponding to the executed vs. not executed malicious intentions groups (experiments 1:text-based and experiment 2: text-based).

Figure 5-28 and Figure 5-29 show the distribution of risk levels of hesitation- vs. motivation-based intentions with the thresholds of 40% and 35% that result in 80% insider threat rejection and 100% insider threat rejection, respectively.

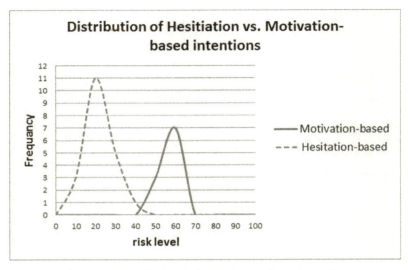

Figure 5-28. Risk levels in the image-based session.

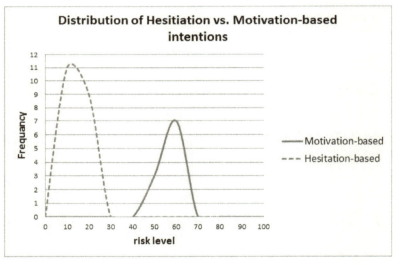

Figure 5-29. Risk levels in the text-based session.

5.2.4 The Potential of IBAC in Preventing Insider Threats (Objective 4)

The results of Objective 3 support the expectations that the first 20 participants' access in Experiment 1 results in low risk compared with the other 10 participants' access in Experiment 2 that results in higher risk.

The value of the intent category as well as the asset value is determined in accordance with ISO27001 Security [103]. In both experiments, the values were assigned based on the level of impact.

Table 12 shows the risk levels in accordance with the impact of an intention category with respect to the confidentiality, integrity and availability (CIA) of information.

Table 12. CIA Risk Assessment Matrix.

CIA Matrix									
C		Low			Medium			High		
I		L	M	H	L	M	H	L	M	H
A	Low	3	4	5	4	5	6	5	6	7
	Medium	4	5	6	5	6	7	6	7	8
	High	5	6	7	6	7	8	7	8	9

In Experiment 1, the intent categories were "Study in Lab," "Help Organize Lab," "Help One Study in a Lab," and "Burn a Lab." The first three categories were assigned as Low-Low-Low with a value of 30, yet the "Burn a Lab" category impacts the CIA and results in High-High-High and a value of 90, which is what may be used in the assessment of risk. Similar to Experiment 1, the intent category impact values can be assigned in Experiment 2.

It is worth noting that an insider is never denied access in the real world at the access control layer in any of the two experiments scenarios, as existing access control systems only rely on identity! The findings in this book support the main hypothesis that states that "*IBAC has the potential to detect and prevent malicious insiders by calculating access risk associated with the detected intent of access and the corresponding motivation level.*"

However, this is the first approach to pursue an intent-based access control, and it is not sufficiently developed to be implemented in real life without further investigations. Further experimentation is required. Open questions remain in the topics of deployment, acceptability, accuracy, usability, and privacy, and others remain in the areas of penetration testing and challenging this approach. Also, addressing numerous types of intent categories in a single access control system is a challenging task. We suggest taking advantage of Role-based Access Control (RBAC). By knowing who is requesting access and their designated role and permissions, we can reduce the number of possible intent categories to test from potentially thousands to a couple of hundreds for that specific role. We can then divide the tasks or permissions into categories of high, medium and low. It is supposed that the high-level possible permissions are lower in number than any of the medium-level or low-level tasks. This reduces the number of possible intent categories or tasks that can be abused from hundreds to few possible intentions. The design of the categories of intentions depends on what the organization wants to protect. If an organization wants to protect everything, this makes the design complex and very complicated. If an organization requires protecting only a selected number of their main resources, then the design is manageable. It is recommended in best practices that an organization pinpoints the most important parts, equipment, commands, and resources and assigning clearance levels. Then, the intent category designer can develop the IBAC system to protect those specific resources whether the protection is by detecting malicious intentions and deny access based on that or simply by allowing access only if the detected intention matches the role of the individual.

Table 13 shows the participants and the intent detection possibility using P300, as well as the motivation level and the total risk, with a 90% intent impact in both experiments

Table 13. Risk data of the 20 participants in Experiment 1 and the 10 participants in Experiment 2.

Participants Ex 1	Intention Detected	Motivation Level (IntM)	Total Risk (R)
1	Yes	0.23	0.207
2	Yes	0.26	0.234
3	Yes	0.25	0.225
4	Yes	0.35	0.315
5	Yes	0.29	0.261
6	Yes	0.3	0.27
7	Yes	0.23	0.207
8	Yes	0.36	0.324
9	Yes	0.23	0.207
10	Yes	0.26	0.234
11	Yes	0.385	0.3465
12	Yes	0.19	0.171
13	Yes	0.29	0.261
14	Yes	0.19	0.171
15	Yes	0.275	0.2475
16	Yes	0.395	0.3555
17	Yes	0.21	0.189
18	Yes	0.32	0.288
19	Yes	0.43	0.387
20	Yes	0.5	0.45
Participants Ex 2	**Intention Detected**	**Motivation Level (IntM)**	**Total Risk (R)**
21	Yes	0.62	0.558
22	Yes	0.65	0.585
23	Yes	0.5	0.45
24	Yes	0.55	0.495
25	Yes	0.45	0.405
26	Yes	0.63	0.567
27	Yes	0.66	0.594
28	Yes	0.59	0.531
29	Yes	0.57	0.513
30	Yes	0.6	0.54

Assuming that the intent category value is similar for all participants with a value of 90%, a two-tailed t-test reports the calculated access risk of 30 participants using the IBAC system with participants who did not execute their intentions (M = 0.26, SD = 0.005) compared with participant who executed their intentions (M = 0.52, SD = 0.003, p ≤ 0.00005.

This supports the hypothesis and suggests that there exists a difference between users with malicious intentions who have low motivation and users with malicious intentions who have high motivation when using the IBAC system.

Analysis of Variance (ANOVA) also suggests a difference between the risk between the two groups with P < 0.0005.

5.2.5   Summary of Findings

In this chapter, Objectives 1, 2 and 3 have been achieved and the two supporting hypotheses have been supported. The details are presented below:

Statistics suggested a difference between intended vs. non-intended actions when recording and analyzing the EEG signals when viewing an image that represents vs. does not represent an intention ($p \leq 0.05$). Objective 1, to adopt and adapt P300-based CIT to accurately detect intentions of access using involuntary physiological signals by exploiting a subject's self-knowledge about an intention using P300-based CIT, has been achieved with an accuracy of 100% using Feature Set 3 when applying the classifiers SVM, Nearest Neighbor, or Random Forest in both experiments' data, with 30 participants in total. This supports Hypothesis 1, which states:

Intention of access can be computed using human physiological signals generally and brain signals specifically by exploiting the self-knowledge existence of intentions.

Furthermore, statistics suggested a difference between the P300 amplitude of participants in Experiment 1 compared with participants in Experiment 2 when viewing images that represent intended actions ($p \leq 0.0005$). Since Experiment 1's participants' intended actions were not executed, as participants showed hesitation in carrying out their intentions, vs. Experiment 2's participants' intended actions being executed as participants showed motivation in carrying out their intentions, this suggests the difference in motivation. Objective 2, to detect the likelihood of an intention to be executed by detecting the intention motivation level using P300, has been achieved. This supports Hypothesis 2, which states:

Motivation detection is possible using human physiological signals generally and brain signals specifically.

The above objectives and hypotheses deliver the intention category and the probability of execution, and serve as the two inputs to calculate the risk level. Also, the above objectives address the possibility of intention detection, which is the main component in Intent-based Access Control (IBAC).

The IBAC system shows the potential in granting Experiment 1 participants access, but denying Experiment 2 participants access. This is because the risk levels of each group show the possibility of setting a threshold value to separate them; however, it is left to the asset owner to decide based on the detected risk of access whether to grant or deny a user access. When achieving Objective 3, to design and test IBAC and to calculate access risk level by building an IBAC system that grants or denies access based on the calculated risk, and applying the calculated risk to all 30 participants using the IBAC system, statistics suggested a difference between Experiment 1 participants' risk level compared with Experiment 2 participants' risk level ($p \leq 0.0005$). The main objective, *to study the potential of using Intent-based Access Control (IBAC) in detecting and preventing malicious insiders*, has been achieved by reporting the risk of access on both experiments' data with 30 participants in total. This supports the main hypothesis, which states:

Main Hypothesis: *Intent-based Access Control (IBAC) has the potential to detect and prevent malicious insiders by calculating access risk associated with the detected intent of access and the corresponding motivation level.*

5.3   Discussion

In this section, a discussion is provided to address the usability, acceptability, privacy concerns, various possibilities of IBAC deployment, limitations, implications, and advantages of IBAC.

5.3.1 IBAC Usability

Since the IBAC system mainly relies on brain signals in order to detect intentions of access and the corresponding motivation level in order to calculate the access risk, there exists a concern of usability. The usability concern is in the form of acquiring brain signals, the intent detection time, and the accuracy of the detection.

Usability is addressed by developing a non-intrusive method of acquiring brain signals. This is achieved by the development of the sensing technology. In the past decade, acquiring brain signals has changed from requiring the use of implanted electrodes via surgical operations to the usage of gel-based or water-based non-invasive electrodes. The advancements in sensing technology have made it possible to detect mental states using as few as only 1 electrode. Wireless-based solutions require less than 2 seconds of setup time, compared with the usage of wire-based sets of 64 or 128 electrodes, with an associated setup time that lasts for more than an hour. Using the Emotiv EEG headset, setup time is about 2 minutes since the headset requires saline solution. Currently, the advancements in sensing technology have made it possible to acquire brain signals using stamp-like electrodes known as BioStamp, which is a light, small, and wireless biosignal sensor. Therefore, brain signals will soon be able to be acquired remotely, as we see currently with ECG signals using a method called Eulerian Video Magnification [104]. Advancements in the sensing technology make the usability of IBAC much more likely. At present, BioStamp in some deployments would be best to employ to overcome the usability concerns of using an EEG headset, they are best in some deployments. BioStamp [105], as shown in Figure 5-30, is an example of how the usability of IBAC can be achieved.

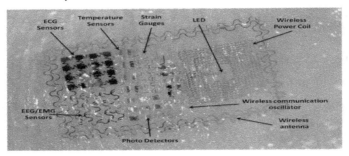

Figure 5-30. BioStamp, a light, stretchable sensor for EEG, ECG and other a bio-signals

[105]

The intent detection accuracy as described in this book reached 100% of intents correctly detected; however, the experiment was conducted in a controlled environment. Further experiments in non-controlled environments may affect the intent detection accuracy. Also, the intent detection time will need to be improved in future work, since the detection of an intent from four possible intentions that takes over 1 minute impacts the usability of the system.

In the IBAC system, we anticipated a usability challenge in using Emotiv EEG, as it requires a saline solution to be applied on each electrode prior to usage. Emotiv Insight [106], as shown in Figure 5-31, is a dry sensor solution that is being developed by Emotiv, which shows promise. Since the P300 signal mainly originates in the center of the scalp, and since Emotiv EPOC does not have a central electrode although it is capable of detecting P300 peaks, we anticipate that using Emotiv Insight would enhance the detection of P300 peaks in fewer trials, which may result in faster detection time and better intent detection accuracy. Emotiv Insight includes a Pz location electrode, which is known to be in the area where the P300 peak is generated.

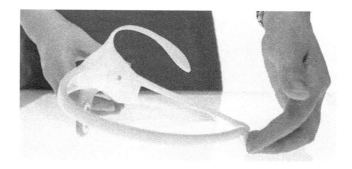

Figure 5-31. Emotiv Insight device [106].

5.3.2 IBAC Acceptability (User's Perspective)

Since IBAC relies on brain signals, user acceptability is affected by a number of factors: 1) brain sensors, 2) privacy concerns, and 3) intent detection time, which influences usability. The brain sensors issue is an acceptability concern, especially if the sensors are attached constantly, as when using BioStamps. From the psychological perspective, people might not be comfortable knowing that their thoughts are being sent elsewhere for processing. Educating users on how IBAC works could assist in improving user acceptability; however, before deploying the technology, it is highly recommended to discuss the legal aspects of this technology and to acquire user's consent. In the case of IBAC, signals are only acquired at the time of access being requested, and not at all times.

The advancements in sensing and wearable technology could help to address acceptability, especially if brain signals are acquired from remote locations, similarly to closed-circuit television (CCTV) monitoring cameras that exist everywhere and that are widely accepted. This acceptance is a result of not being connected with sensors, as we subconsciously believe that our privacy is not breached.

Also, people normally accept biometric one-time authentication measures, but not continuous monitoring. However, security research has studied the issue of one-time authentication and has already moved toward research in continuous authentication. One example is [17], which addresses an open session hijacking possibility in one-time authentication.

The acceptability of IBAC is affected by the fact that the technology does not provide protection to the user, but instead offers protection from the user's intentions. This concern is addressed in changing the perspective of detection so that it deters an insider form abusing his or her privileges instead of convicting him or her. The detection of an insider can be viewed from two perspectives: 1) to convict an insider before they perform the malicious activity, and 2) to alert an insider that any further activity will be logged and reported to their manager. The first perspective is usually not accepted, since people can argue that such technology convicts a person of an activity that has not yet been performed, and the result is rejection of such technology. However, the second perspective is more accepted, since it alerts an insider that he or she has raised a red flag and that he or she will be convicted if any malicious activity is attempted. The alert component can be replaced or added to by applying Segregation of Duty (SoD), which becomes enforced in case a flag is raised. Such perspective alerts an insider and results in a reconsideration of the consequences before a malicious activity is executed. It may also persuade an employee not to commit the crime.

The acceptability of such technology also depends on educating users that the acquired signals are not personally identifiable information (PII), since IBAC does not record or save the signals or compare them to a user's template, but rather analyzes it on the fly for specific signatures, the existence of P300 signals, and to determine the tested intent categories. If any user accepts biometric measurements such as fingerprints, iris, or face, even though these impose on users' privacy and the recorded templates are PII, they should accept IBAC, as it does not invade privacy at all, as it is designed with privacy in mind, unlike other biometric measurements. When privacy is addressed, it improves the user acceptability aspect of IBAC as well. The privacy aspect is addressed in the next section.

5.3.3 IBAC Privacy Issues

Privacy is an important factor of acceptability. A robust and secure system that invades users' privacy is not acceptable and therefore not usable. Taking this into consideration, IBAC was designed with privacy in mind, following the *privacy by design* principle [107]. Privacy by design includes a proactive, rather than a reactive, approach to prevent and not to remediate possible privacy breaches. It also includes a *privacy by default* aspect and privacy embedded into the design, as well as respect for users' privacy. IBAC does not record the user's information or brain signals. It does not require enrollment and template generation of a user, as it is not an identity verification system. IBAC detects the existence of knowledge of a plan. Depending on the plan or the intent, the risk level is calculated. However, since the technology relies on brain signals, people do not trust and accept such technology without prior knowledge of facts. Yet, the IBAC does not rely on recorded and stored brain signals. Thus, IBAC does not impact the privacy of a user. It is the phobia about new technology that makes us believe that this will invade our privacy, especially without prior knowledge of how it works. Bio-signals always encounter the issue of privacy concerns. *How will it be possible to protect the user's information?* has been a question frequently posed. However, in contrast to traditional identity-based biometrics, where a template of bio-features such as face, fingerprint, iris, and voice is saved for future matching, IBAC does not require maintaining any user records, and therefore it does not impact users' privacy. IBAC does not recognize individuals, but instead recognizes the existence of a plan to commit maleficence. Therefore, the privacy concerns are lower than in any other biometric system.

Identity-based biometric systems invade privacy because they were not designed with privacy in mind. Previous research demonstrated the possibility of reconstructing an image of a face and a fingerprint using stored users' templates. In 2007, Cappelli *et al.* [108] reconstructed fingerprints using stored users' templates by reverse engineering minute template data from commercial fingerprint systems, as seen in Figure 5-32. Reconstructing fingerprints imposes a huge impact on users' privacy, as it allows attackers to create gelatin fingerprints of real individuals to be used maliciously. This may allow an attacker to authenticate to a system as an authorized user or to commit a crime and implicate the individual whose fingerprints have been reconstructed.

**Fingerprint reconstruction from
minutiae template (Cappelli et al, 2007)**

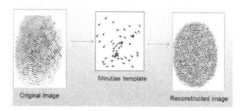

Figure 5-32. Reconstruction of a fingerprint image from a template [108]

Similarly to fingerprints, facial images have been reconstructed from templates. Mohanty [109] showed in 2007 how face recognition biometric systems invade users' privacy, as seen in Figure 5-33. This represents a significant compromise of the users' privacy, as their images can be reconstructed.

Face reconstruction from a commercial off-the-shelf facial recognition system

Figure 5-33. Reconstruction of a face image from a template [109].

IBAC does not record templates of users, and therefore it is not susceptible to the threat of template reconstruction. It is also not susceptible as well to the following privacy attacks that impact identity-based biometric systems, including:

- Function creep, which is a term used to describe the collection of data for a specific purpose but then using it for another purpose. This is a privacy concern, but it does not apply to IBAC, as IBAC does not save the EEG signals to compute the risk of access unless it is redesigned to do so. This is because EEG signals can result in identification of individuals if templates are created, yet this is not a facet of the IBAC system, but rather an EEG-based access control.

- Linkage of databases, which is done to connect multiple systems together. However, this privacy concern does not apply to IBAC, since this technology does not store any user's data unless it is redesigned to do so for other purposes unrelated to this book.

- Expanded surveillance, which involves employing the user templates for surveillance, does not apply to IBAC, as this technology does not store any user's information.

- Loss of personal control, which is a privacy risk a user faces when his or her template is used in function creep or expanded surveillance. This is especially a concern for biometric data, which are PII and which do not change over time. However, this does not apply to IBAC, as this technology does not store any users' data.

- Misuse of data (data breach, ID fraud, theft) does not apply to IBAC, as no data are stored, and therefore cannot be stolen.

5.3.4 IBAC Deployment

IBAC deployment depends significantly on how it is intended to be used. In the case of general public usage, IBAC could be used as a standalone system. However, IBAC could also be used and combined with known identity-based measures including Role-based Access Control (RBAC). IBAC could be used by connecting sensors such as BioStamp, or by placing an EEG headset in place.

IBAC could be used to secure facilities such as a physical access control systems or might be used to secure computer systems and files from malicious insiders. It can also be used in airports where an entry visa holder (authorized to access) but with malicious intents should be rejected access in order to prevent an incident from occurring.

IBAC as a Standalone System

IBAC works as a standalone access control model in specific deployment scenarios when identity is not essential, such as in access to stadiums, theaters, malls, offices, or other public spaces. Current access control systems are only deployed to verify the existence of a token or ticket that is purchased, which is certainly not a valid input to detect risk of malicious access. As a result, assessment of the risk of malicious access in such scenarios of current access control systems is not even implemented. IBAC addresses this need by detecting the intention of access, regardless of identity or the existence of an access token. IBAC works as a standalone model, as depicted in Figure 5-34. As determination of identity is not essential in locations of public access, one needs to implement a system that detects the possibility of malicious intention or abuse of privilege. The intention detection system can be deployed as a standalone system that does not require user enrollments, and where the burden of user account management is eliminated. However, the IBAC system needs to be further improved to address the limitations of the new technology. Limitations are provided in Section 5.3.5.

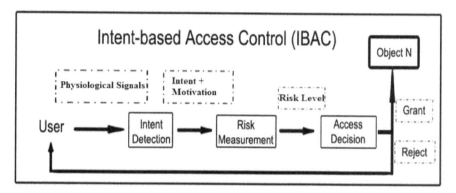

Figure 5-34. Intent-based Access Control (IBAC) standalone design.

IBAC Combined With an Identity-based Access Control System

The advantages of IBAC are shown in overcoming the weaknesses that current access control systems suffer from. Existing access control systems do not take into consideration the insider threat factor, by basing the access decision solely on identity. IBAC addresses this vulnerability and assesses the user's intention as a risk factor. Therefore, existing access control systems, when accompanied by IBAC, become much more sensitive to insider threats and address these threats as a risk factor. As a result, when IBAC accompanies existing access control systems, the insider threat becomes addressed and the security level becomes higher. IBAC works on top of existing access control models such as RBAC/HBAC, as depicted in

Figure 5-35. Deployment could be accomplished as a physical access method, such as access to a facility, to a car, or to computer files.

In some deployments in which an identity is required, determining the intention of a user can play the role of a second layer of defense. In such a case, the detection of malicious intentions can be used to thwart threats.

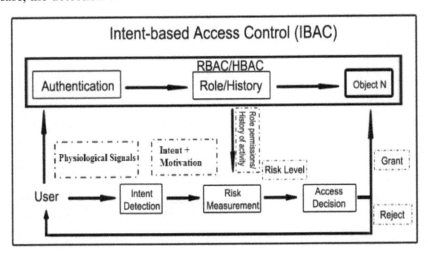

Figure 5-35. IBAC system combined with RBAC/HBAC models.

5.3.5 IBAC Challenges and Limitations

The work presented in this book is the first effort made to achieve an intent-based access control system, and might not sufficiently be mature to be implemented in the real world without further investigations. Additional experimentation is required. Necessary experiments involve the topics of deployment, acceptability, accuracy, usability, and privacy. Further testing might include penetration testing and challenging the approach.

Challenges to improve the IBAC technology include:

- Strengthening the Intent Detection component to be robust against attacks and special cases, such as emotions, illness, distraction, and environmental noise.

- Improving the Motivation Detection component to be accurate. This might be accomplished by combining other technologies such as social network data, behavioral data, and other methods of motivation detection.

- Enhancing the Risk Assessment component by assessing risk using multiple resources of data including the user's role and history.

- Strengthening the Decision-Making component by adding other sources of information before making an access decision.

- Addressing system performance, usability, acceptability, privacy, deployment, challenges, limitations and implications.

- Deploying the system in real-world scenarios to assess its robustness as a step in assessing the feasibility of IBAC.

- Designing penetration tests on the Intention, Motivation, Sensor, Risk Assessment, and Decision-Making components and suggesting solutions to each component.

5.3.6 IBAC Implications

New technologies provide solutions to detect and prevent problems; however, implications may arise as a result of the existence of these new technologies. Addressing implications is essential and requires first identifying them.

The existence of an IBAC system is helpful in answering the question "Why is an access being requested?" It provides an automatic re-evaluation of trust in a trusted and authorized entity; however, it should be sufficiently mature that there exist no false positives, since denying a legitimate access could result in catastrophic incidents as much as allowing a malicious insider access, and may be worse. Therefore, this technology requires further investigation before it is deployed.

IBAC as a new technology presents a number of implications that need to be addressed carefully. Some of those implications are social and others are psychological; both affect the environment in which the system is deployed. Those social and psychological implications are affected by the decision-making component of denying or granting access based on intentions. As a result, there is a need to define the meaning of when a malicious intent is detected, as well as to design strategies related to how to manage users who have been denied access due to the detection of malicious intent. The definitions and strategies strongly depend on the categories of the intents that are tested, the environment in which IBAC is deployed, the resources that are protected, as well as the types of users who use the system (e.g. high-level and low-level employees). As a general rule, the definition of the detection of malicious intent is a protection for both the resources and users from being tampered with or tampered by, respectively. The strategies at this stage of the technology may begin with targeted monitoring of users when malicious intents are detected, until further tests are carried out to demonstrate the feasibility, stability and accuracy of the system.

The implications and recommendations about how to avoid or fix these challenges are given below and divided based on the user's perspective and the administrator's perspective:

The User's Perspective:

Users need to understand that the objective of IBAC is not to accuse them of having a malicious intent, but to prevent them from abusing their privileges or committing maleficence. In that case, IBAC serves as a protection to users from themselves. By understanding this objective, we address the acceptability aspect of using the technology and avoid psychological and social implications, especially when the results of IBAC are kept private.

Implications highly depend on the actions taken after detecting malicious intents. Therefore, the actions need to be designed carefully. IBAC can be used to monitor and investigate specific users who have been denied access due to the detection of malicious intents.

The accuracy of the system is a very important aspect, as the decision-making component, actions, and resulting implications depend on it. FAR and FRR need to be reduced, and if these factors are not reduced, they require, at a minimum, to be considered before making a judgment. Further tests on IBAC may address the accuracy of the system and consider the implications that may occur as a result. When a user is detected to have a malicious intent, whether correct or incorrect, he or she can anticipate that a flag was raised and that his or her activity is now being monitored. This deters users who have a malicious intent from executing their attacks.

Since IBAC is a pre-crime technology, as it detects the existence of a plan to be executed, it may not be acceptable in its current form, unless the actions taken related to when an intent is detected are kept private for the benefit of the user. Implications also exist in the area of fooling the system, which is a concern similar to those of biometric systems. Penetration tests are needed to be executed to address such concerns.

The IBAC Administrator's Perspective:

Since two of the profiles of insider threats are considered high-level users, including managers, administrators, scientists, and engineers, it is important that the system is designed with privacy in mind when combining IBAC to an identity-based solution in order to keep the identities of detected users who have malicious intents private until proving that they are abusing their privileges. An action can then be taken to identify the user and initiate a process in which the abuse of privileges is detected.

Management may respond based on monitoring the user's activity until detecting that an insider attack is occurring. Until the system is tested in real-world settings, the monitoring of users should be the main action performed. After refinement and demonstration of the stability and accuracy of the system, the system may lock accounts and report incidents.

False positives should have the highest priority to be minimized compared with false negatives, since preventing access to a legitimate user might incur high risk imposed by the designed system. False negatives, if minimized to a certain degree, even if not fully eliminated, would be accepted, since IBAC serves as the only access control that can minimize false negatives in the insider threat context compared with other methods. However, having users informed that IBAC has been implemented may reduce any suspension of an insider attack. This may be fixed by educating the insider threat team about the accuracy of the system. Although the log of the IBAC model for detected intentions and corresponding motivation levels may be abused by management, the IBAC system may be used to detect the intentions of requesting access to the logs of the system and either grant or denied access in case the access request is to abuse privileges.

5.3.7 IBAC Advantages

The main advantage that IBAC offers in comparison with the current access control models is the ability to test the trustworthiness of subjects requesting access, regardless of their identity, since an identity is never an indicator of good or malicious intentions of access.

The advantages of IBAC over current access control systems include the characteristics that IBAC is:

- [ ] the only access control system designed to detect and prevent insider threats.
- [ ] the only access control system using intention and motivation of access to calculate access risk.
- [ ] the only access control system that does not need to record a user's template.
- [ ] designed with privacy in mind, as detailed in Section 5.3.3.
- [ ] secure against identity-based access control systems' privacy attacks including:
  - o Function creep
  - o Linkage of databases
  - o Expanded surveillance
  - o Loss of personal control
  - o Misuse of data
- [ ] secure against identity-based access control systems' attacks on the storage component, as it does not record data or match against a template.

☐ a risk-based access control that assesses the risk of access from the insider threat point of view, while current identity-based access control systems target outsider threats.

Comparing IBAC to RBAC Using the Experimental Details:

In experiments 1 and 2, users would have had the ability to gain access if provided credentials (username and password) with a guest role to access the lab and laptop. To compare RBAC with IBAC, we notice that the RBAC model did not calculate any insider threat possibility, since the insider threat is not considered when designing an RBAC model in the case of abuse of privileges. All participants of both experiments were to be granted access; however, IBAC was able to detect 100% of tested insider incidents, and based on the calculated risk level, IBAC was able to detect and prevent the insider threats. This comparison reveals that RBAC is designed to deter outsider threats with minimum consideration of insider threats. RBAC can prevent a user from committing maleficence that he or she does not have the permissions to engage in; however, it does not prevent an insider from committing maleficence using his or her existing privileges. In contrast, IBAC was able to detect and prevent insiders from committing maleficence with the privileges they have, as IBAC bases the access risk on the intent category, asset, and motivation levels. IBAC, when combined with RBAC, delivers better results than either methods individually, as IBAC risk calculations will accompany the role as well as the access risk calculation requirements.

In the next chapter, Chapter 6, a discussion will be provided of the future work required to strengthen the IBAC system, including improving the intention, motivation, risk assessment, and decision-making components, along with further tests to address the feasibility of IBAC.

CHAPTER 6. Future Work

One of the main aspects of this book entails conducting research in Intention Detection, Motivation Detection, and, most significantly, Non-Identity-based Access Control to combat insider threats. This book also suggests future work to strengthen the IBAC system and addresses its limitations. This chapter explores possible future research work in the aforementioned fields.

6.1 Intention Detection

Intention detection can be improved by studying the factors that affect the P300 signal and addressing the accuracy and speed of intent detection.

In the detection of intentions of access, we presented images on a screen, where each image lasted for 1 second for a total of 16 trials required (16 seconds per intention); however, that resulted in a long duration to test multiple intentions, which affected the acceptability and usability of the technology. Also, we present specific intention-related images, which results in detecting specific intentions as opposed to detecting general direction of intentions (e.g. malicious intentions vs. good intention).

Future research questions become necessary to address including the ability to detect general directions of intentions instead of specific intentions. For example, in experiment 1, if participants have an intention to damage a lab, would the system be able to detect any intention related to damaging a lab, including setting a lab on fire? Also, developing a methodology in designing best stimuli, designing a system component to differentiate between futuristic vs. past knowledge, designing methods to discover and exploit the vulnerabilities in the IBAC system, designing countermeasure methods to strengthen the IBAC model from discovered vulnerabilities, comparing different types of stimuli (image-text-audio), detecting emotions and signs of illness and researching their impact on the accuracy of the system in detecting intentions of access and investigating the accuracy of the system when it is used for a period of time.

Some concerns regarding the analysis and experiment design of an ERP related experiment are addressed by Luck [110], including: if target is always preceded by nontarget, and nontarget baseline is contaminated by overlap from previous P300 signal. Then we may use a completely random sequence or during averaging, we exclude non-targets preceded by targets. If peak amplitude is biased by the number of trials, we can use mean amplitude. Further, if brightness manipulation has the side effect of changing the sensory components, we may control the experiment to show that brightness per se does not impact P300 amplitude. As this book explores the usage of text-based vs. image-based data to measure the effect of bright images, future work should include confirming the results by having a control population consisting of people with good intent or no intent of access while using the system. Finally, if subjects may be in a different state of arousal during bright and dim blocks, we may mix brightness within blocks.

Some of the challenges can be addressed using the Complex Trial Protocol (CTP).

6.1.1 Complex Trial Protocol (CTP)

The Complex Trial Protocol (CTP) consists of a *probe* that is followed by either a *target* or *non-target* stimulus with a 1,100–1,550 *ms* interval. It was shown in [111] that the CTP protocol overcomes countermeasures of knowing what the probes are, which is a vulnerability of other trial protocols, such as the trial protocol of randomly showing probes, targets, and non-target stimuli. CTP requires a user to press the same button when a probe or a non-target is presented. If the P300 amplitude is higher in the *probe* category than in the *target* or *non-target* categories, this indicates knowledge of the probe information, and concealed information is then detected. Figure 6-1 shows the CTP protocol starting from left to right.

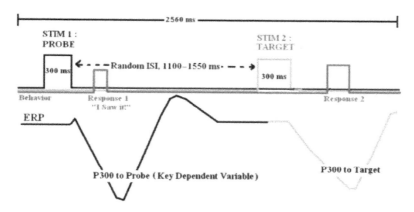

Figure 6-1. Complex Trial Protocol
[112]

While CTP shows promise to mitigate different strategies of fooling the P300 classifier, it is not practical to be used in real-world settings. As a result, techniques to adapt the protocol to be faster and not require the user's compliance should be addressed in future work.

This book only addresses the potential of the described technology. We are not proposing a full solution to be implemented in its current form, but rather, we are proposing a new approach and method that can be used in combination with existing solutions to strengthen the mitigation of insider threats. The above questions are necessary components of future work to address the feasibility of this technology in the Intent Detection component of IBAC.

Furthermore, novel approaches in intent detection are desirable. Some novel approaches might involve using remote micro-behavioral measurements that may address the acceptability of intent detection and that may be comparable to the use of EEG signals.

Further, since the device that was used in this book is the Emotiv EEG headset, future work may include using other headsets and testing the accuracy using the intent detection algorithm and if there is a necessity to improve on the algorithm to be device independent.

Also, acquiring EEG signals from remote sources, without touching the user's scalp, is a very important research step in the sensory technology for addressing the acceptability and usability of the system. However, this has not yet been accomplished.

6.2 Motivation Detection

Motivation detection has been studied by [85] as well as being addressed in this book; however, novel approaches in detecting motivation related to intention of access are desirable. Some approaches might target the facial expressions and emotions related to intentions of access. The results might be comparable to the usage of EEG signals to detect motivation of access. Can ECG, GSR, or body temperature provide useful information about motivation levels? This question, and many others, must be examined to select the best motivation detection method to be used with IBAC.

Future research questions include:

1- Determining the difference between target ERP and non-target ERP signals in the case of amplitude to measure motive, instead of only measuring the ERP of targets as a motivation measure.

2- Finding the difference between 0-50 *ms* highest μV compared with 200-500 *ms* highest μV amplitude in the target category, where the signal is at its peak as a motivation measure.

3- Measuring the deviation rate in 0-50 *ms* highest μV compared with 200-500 *ms* highest μV in the target category, where the signal is at its peak as a motivation measure.

4- Comparing the above three motivation measurements and reporting the best approach among them.

6.3 IBAC Improvement

The IBAC system can be improved from different perspectives including, but not limited to, improving the Intent Detection component (Section 6.1), Motivation Detection component (Section 6.2), Risk Assessment component (Section 6.3.2), and Decision-Making component (Section 6.3.3).

6.3.1 Intent and Motivation Improvement

As stated in Sections 6.1 and 6.2, the IBAC system does not necessarily have to employ only EEG signals. If any other method of detecting intentions of access, as well as detecting motivation related intentions, is discovered, such a method could replace and possibly improve the accuracy of the detection of insider threats. There is also a possibility to combine the methods that detect intent and motivation, and to design a component in the system to make a decision based on these findings.

6.3.2 Risk Assessment

The risk assessment component currently relies on the intent category risk, intent detection, motivation level, and asset value to calculate the overall risk and asset loss. However, combining IBAC with an identity-based access control, and especially with HBAC and RBAC, may improve the accuracy of the risk assessment component significantly. Knowing the role of a user to be an administrator addresses the risk calculation component differently than if the role of a user is a low-level employee; similarly, the history of that employee can be considered. If an administrator is using a sensitive command that has not been used previously, the risk is different than when using a command that has been used daily. The risk assessment component may also take into consideration the social characteristics of a user, by following his or her social media accounts and analyzing the emotions of the user or any threat that may be inferred. Furthermore, environmental sensors may provide information to assess the risk. When an administrator is executing a command to delete sensitive data in the middle of the night or while the fire alarm has been activated, risk may be different than when deleting sensitive data in the normal working hours or environment.

6.3.3 Decision-Making

The Decision-Making component may be improved by considering the history of decisions that were made for a particular user. Also, combining IBAC with RBAC provides another layer of analysis when making the decision. Knowing the role of a user may assist in delivering concise access decisions. Further, combining IBAC with an environmentally aware system when making the access decision is important, as it adds more intelligence to the Decision-Making component before making an access decision.

6.3.4 Further Tests

Acceptability and usability tests are essential to address by employing surveys before, during, and after use of the system. Observational tests of the users and system responses are also necessary. Also, testing the feasibility of the system in real deployments is important, as the current research has only tested the potential of the system in a controlled environment, yet real-world situations will not involve such controlled environments. Tests need to be conducted with different emotions, illnesses, distractions, and methods of challenging the sensor component of the system (e.g. a malicious EEG headset that claims to be from a vendor while it is designed to send pre-recorded EEG signal). A solution to such issue is in authenticating the EEG headset using digital certificates.

For example, there is a potential of testing the system in an airport where people are selected randomly, as seen with airport screening technologies such as ProVision. However, it is not a carried explosive that the IBAC system may look for, but rather a travel destination. The system may import the next four hours' possible destinations in the airport and detect where a traveler intends to go. Then, the detected destination intention could be validated with the boarding pass information. Depending on whether the results match the boarding pass, the accuracy of the system in real-world settings can be reported. This experiment may start in a university lab for participants who intend to travel in Canada to detect the province they intend to travel to, and then expand to airport settings to address this emotional aspect in a real-world setting.

6.3.5 Further IBAC Improvements

Designing a framework for the IBAC system is a necessary improvement in order to streamline any development of the system to serve multiple directions of usage. Further, taking advantage of Belief Desire and

Intention (BDI) software model [113], may be beneficial in the design of the framework especially since the BDI model translates desire to motivation and matches the objectives of IBAC system. Furthermore, adding the Trust Computing Base (TCB) [114], which is a part of a system that contains all necessary components to ensure the security of a system, may be a necessary component that addresses the vulnerabilities of the IBAC system.

IBAC can also serve as an identity-based access control method, since EEG signals have been shown to uniquely identify individuals with an accuracy of 97% [48]. This makes the IBAC system not only an insider threat-related system, but also an outsider threat protection system; however, in this case, IBAC impacts on the privacy of users similarly to identity-based access control systems.

Once the challenges and limitations of IBAC are known by developing a penetration test for the system, which should include the sensor side, the risk assessment side, and/or the decision-making side, a mitigation plan should be developed to secure each of the IBAC components. A penetration test is in the form of scanning the system, detecting and exploiting the vulnerabilities in the IBAC system and suggest solutions to each vulnerability. Since IBAC is indeed a biometric system but is not identity-based, it is possible that current mitigation plans in biometric systems of each of the components could map directly to IBAC. Also, a mathematical model for the IBAC system is an important step in improving the understanding of IBAC system since it provides a starting point for evaluating the technology.

IBAC can also serve as a one-time authentication system and lacks the ability to detect developed malicious intents that occur after being legitimately authenticated. For this, we proposed the use of Physiological Signal Monitoring (PSM) [115], a system that detects when a user commits maleficence when the recorded signal (ECG, GSR and skin temperature) deviates abnormally. IBAC plus PSM deliver the Insider Threat Monitoring System (ITMS) as presented in Figure 6-2, where a user is initially authenticated using IBAC and then the system continuously monitors the user's physiological signals. If any abnormal deviation of the signal occurs, IBAC is then used to re-authenticate the intentions of the user.

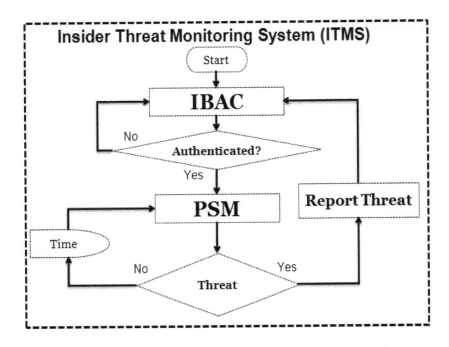

Figure 6-2. ITMS algorithm featuring the IBAC and PSM components.

The PSM system uses the the NeXus-10 MK II from MindMedia [116] as depicted in Figure 6-3. The sensors used are ECG, GSR, and temperature, as shown in Figures 6-(4-6), respectively.

Figure 6-3. NeXus-10 MKII from MindMedia
[116].

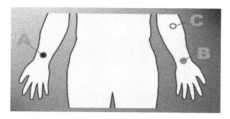

Figure 6-4. NeXus-10 MKII ECG sensor
[116].

Figure 6-5. NeXus-10 MKII GSR sensor
[116].

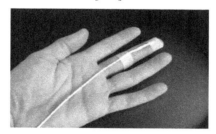

Figure 6-6. NeXus-10 MKII temperature sensor
[116].

The results of testing users during normal vs. malacious activity are shown in Figure 6-7, Figure 6-8 and Figure 6-9 The malacious activities were detected with 100% accuracy using a functional tree classifier. Figure 6-10 shows the signal deviation between the two conditions.

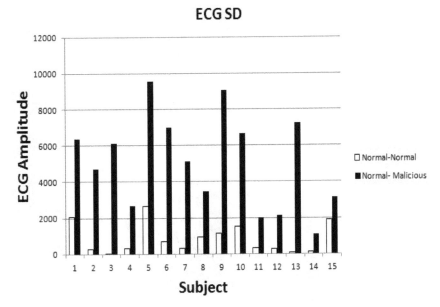

Figure 6-7. ECG amplitude signal deviation among 15 participants in Normal-Normal and Normal-Malicious phases.

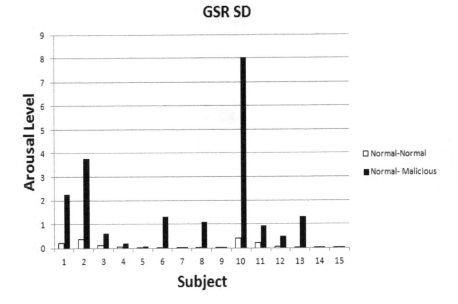

Figure 6-8. GSR signal deviation among 15 participants in Normal-Normal and Normal-Malicious phases.

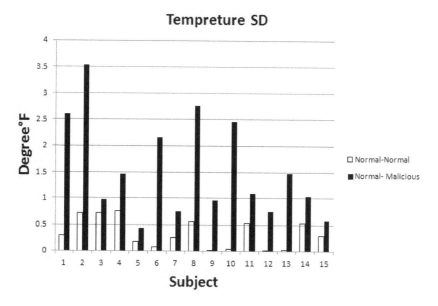

Figure 6-9. Temperature signal deviation among 15 participants in Normal-Normal and Normal-Malicious phases.

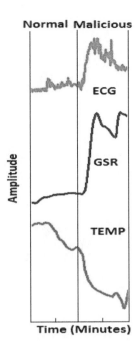

Figure 6-10. Overview of ECG, GSR and TEMP measures in normal and malicious activity.

As this book investigates the potential of IBAC to detect insider threats, there is a need for work to investigate the feasibility of IBAC in real deployments. The feasibility questions are outlined as part of this chapter.

6.4 Non-Identity-based Access Control

Non-identity-based access control is a new field of study that explores new ways to identify why access is being requested instead of who is requesting access, which is one of the contributions of this book. Emotion-based access control (EBAC) [117] is a system that can potentially be combined with IBAC in answering why access is being requested. EBAC detects the levels and types of emotions to determine access decisions.

6.5 Other Research Areas

Trust re-evaluation, human error, advertising, marketing, and gaming are areas that can benefit from detecting an intention and motivation related to that intention.

Trust is an important concept in human relationships. However, trust yields a false sense of security, as trust leads to decreased vigilance toward a threat. Cases related to fraudulent activities and life-threatening incidents highlight the importance and necessity of trust re-evaluation. Trust re-evaluation has been studied over the last decade, yet none of the approaches has targeted the physiological measurements of a trustee, nor does any existing method provide a trustor with a system to detect the intentions of a trustee when providing information to that trustee. Future work includes the design of a human-to-human trust re-evaluation system that provides the trustor with the risk levels of trusting a particular trustee. This could be a cloud-based service that detects the intentions and motivation levels behind the information a trustee provides using the intent and motivation detection components of the Intent-based Access Control (IBAC) model. A trustor is provided with the risk of trusting a trustee; hence, a trustor can make informed decisions about whether or not to trust the trustee and accept the provided information. Further, a certificate of good intentions is granted to a trustee to present to a trustor if the risk levels are determined to be low.

Misplaced trust can result not only in financial losses, but may also extend to life-threatening incidents and homicide. Incidents related to trust using social network platforms including Craigslist, Kijiji, Facebook, Twitter, and Instagram, or any venue in which users may exchange private information such as their location, has cost people not only their money, but also their lives. As stated by CNN [118], "the grisly cutting of a fetus from a woman began with a Craigslist ad about baby clothes for sale." Furthermore, a student was robbed and killed when attempting to sell his car to a person who replied to his Craigslist advertisement [119]. Many similar examples emphasize the need for trust re-evaluation, with possible deployment venues that include social networking platforms and financial organizations. Such trust re-evaluation can detect and prevent trust abuse that may lead to securities fraud among other types of fraud that involve trusting another human being.

In human error research work, IBAC could be adapted to determine whether an action was intentional or a result of an unintentional mistake. IBAC could assist in the advertising field as well, by determining what a user may intend to buy and offer that product to them. Further, IBAC may enhance the gaming industry when providing a game that executes functions based on intentions with an amplitude of that function based on motivation.

The proposed method of intent detection to provide information about planned actions plus motivation detection to predict the likelihood of intent execution serve as improvements of numerous fields of study including disaster prevention planning, incident response planning, and other areas of academic study including marketing, business planning, and advertising.

CHAPTER 7. Conclusions

Insider threat incidents are significantly lower in number compared with outsider attacks, yet the impact of insider threat incidents is catastrophic. Insider threats result in an unbearable risk that exists in all organizations. Existing solutions for the insider threat have limitations that do not fully address this threat. Therefore, in this book, we suggested a novel one-size-fits-all approach for insider threats from the first layer of defense, access control. We proposed an access control system that verifies the intent of access, called Intent-based Access Control (IBAC), instead of detecting the user's identity.

Since the threat is human-based, solutions should target the source of the threat and not rely only on the possible actions; therefore, solutions need to measure human bio-signals in order to detect insider threats.

Since people are aware of their intentions and know whether they are good or malicious, we took advantage of advancements in sensing technology and the BCI field to design an access control system that targets the source of the threat, the insiders. We exploited the user's knowledge about intent to detect intentions using brain signals. Since IBAC is a risk-based access control method, and knowledge about an intention may not indicate the precise risk, we proposed the detection of intent motivation level that corresponds to intent likelihood of execution using brain signal amplitude. Based on the risk level, IBAC's decision-making component denies or grants access. The IBAC system is intended to provide data to support a decision, but should not make a decision on its own. Such decision should be made by understanding risk and setting the decision component to the value that best protects the organization's resources against insider threats.

Our experimental data and statistical results show that there exists the possibility of detecting the intention of access and computing the intent motivation level in an access control model that has the potential of denying access to authorized but malicious insiders. However, the model still requires many improvements to strengthen it and to make it usable, acceptable, and automatic.

171

Other approaches such as emotion detection could be added to the proposed model to assess risk from the emotional perspective. IBAC is a one-time authentication measurement that does not address malicious intents that may be developed after being authenticated; therefore, there exists a need for continuous monitoring of intents. It should be noted that our study is a new approach for authentication methods that is non-identity based, and that employs the user's intention of access to determine whether access should be granted or denied by computing the risk of access. Like any new approach, there are plenty of challenges, improvements, and questions that need to be investigated and answered using experimental methods. These challenges and improvements include:

a) Improvements in the Intent Detection component: This book mainly utilizes the P300 signal to detect intentions of access. This approach can be improved by addressing the stimuli selection criteria including the size, brightness, content, and relevance of stimuli. Also, the intent detection approach can be improved by addressing the signal pre-processing and processing aspects, as well as the possibility of distractions as a result of internal or external sources such as illness or emotions. Further research in challenging the intent detection component is required, such challenge may include a user blinking with a high frequency, closing his or her eyes, or paying attention to a non-related item on the screen is required, along with proposed methodologies for mitigating these attacks. Research to investigate whether it is preferable to use general or specific intentions to be detected is needed, as well. Identifying other intent detection methods, such as behavioral approaches, and comparing them with physiological approaches is preferred to select the optimal approach.

b) Improvements in the Motivation Detection component: Investigation of further methods for motivation detection are needed, which may include the analysis of GSR or ECG signals, or eye pattern movements.

c) Improvements in the Risk Assessment component: These may benefit from combining IBAC with current access control systems such as RBAC or HBAC. Knowing the role of a user and his or her history may assist in assessing risk with a higher level of accuracy. Also, including an environmentally aware system may provide another level of sensation when measuring the risk of access.

d) Improvements in the Decision-Making component: The Decision-Making component can be improved by taking into consideration the previous risk levels of a specific user when making a new decision.

e) Further tests include assessing and improving the acceptability, usability, privacy, and compliance of the proposed system. Acceptability may be tested and improved by discovering the aspects of the system that can be made easier to interact with. This includes the possibility of remote acquisition of EEG signals. Usability may be significantly improved if the system is acceptable and has low False Acceptance Rate and False Rejection Rate values, with an acceptable access decision response time

ABOUT THE AUTHOR

Abdulaziz Almehmadi received the Bachelor's degree in computer science, the Master's degree in information technology security, with a specialty in biometrics, the Ph.D. in computer science with a specialty in Access Control and Biometrics from King Abdulaziz University, Jeddah, Saudi Arabia, and University of Ontario Institute of Technology, Ontario, Canada in 2007, 2010, and 2016 respectively. He is currently the Vice-Dean for Graduate Studies and Research and an Assistant Professor at the Faculty of Computers and IT, University of Tabuk.

Abdulaziz Almehmadi, PhD
4lmehmadi@gmail.com

Appendix 1: Experiments Pseudo Code

Screenshot of testbench while recording EEG signals:

The below figure shows sent markers from the C# program, which involves images flashing, and EEG signals being recorded using *testbench*.

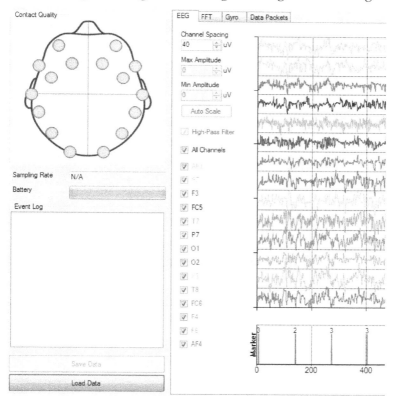

Testbench recorded EEG signals while viewing intent category-related images.

Pseudo Code of Experiments:

Experiment Start

```
{

    Start timer for 60 seconds \\ baseline recording

    Send marker to testbench.exe \\ a marker is sent to state when
baseline recording has started.

        if ( 60 seconds timer is done)

        {

            Send marker to testbench.exe \\ a maker is sent to state when
        baseline has ended.

            Stop timer

        }

        Start timer for 64 seconds

        {

                For every second

                {

                    if (an image is shown)

                    {

                        Hide the image.

                        Show image from one of the four intent
                    categories.

                        Send a unique marker to testbench.exe for each
                    intent category image.

                    }

                }

        }

} \\ experiment is done.
```

Appendix 2: List of Publications

1) The State of the Art in Electroencephalogram and Access Control [120]. Published in *Proceedings of the 3rd* International Conference on Communications and Information Technology (ICCIT'13)

"Electroencephalogram (EEG) is the recorded electrical signals generated by the brain. EEG signals can be recorded using electrodes placed on the scalp. The recorded signal is usually filtered and analyzed for feature extractions. These features have proven to be accurate enough for user authentication. This study provides a deep analysis of different approaches of EEG user authentication, their strength, and weaknesses and draws a conclusion on future directions in this field." This paper provided a literature review of using EEG as a biometric measure, which was used in this book in Section 2.4.1, Electroencephalogram (EEG) Robustness in Patterns of Individual Differences and Similarities.

2) Authorized! Access Denied, Unauthorized! Access Granted [117]. Published in *Proceedings of the 7th International Conference on Security of Information and Networks'* 13.

"Existing access control systems are mostly identity-based. However, such access control systems impose risks because recognized identity is not essentially an interpretation of good intentions of access. On the other hand, an un-identified individual might request access to suppress damage or prevent a catastrophic incident from happening. To address the limitation of current access control systems, we propose an access control method that is based on feelings which relates an access decision to the current detected emotion of the user, and map it to a category of feelings. Feelings categories are either negative resulting in denying access, or positive leading to access being granted. The proposed emotion-based access control (EBAC) mechanism adds the feelings sensation to the access control machines by analyzing the requesters' current brain signals at the time of access request to detect their current emotions, and then grants or denies access." This paper proposed Emotion-based Access Control (EBAC) and the concept of Non-Identity based Access Control. These concepts are used in this book to design of IBAC system.

3) A Tweet of the Mind: Automated Emotion Detection for Social Media Using Brain Wave Pattern Analysis [121]. Published in SocialCom'13.

"While millions of individuals around the globe use social media every second to disseminate, in some form, their emotions and experiences, there are still some situational challenges these individuals face while trying to share experience over social media. This work introduces the idea of using a Brain Computer Interface device to detect human emotion, which is then paired with geo-location information and automatically posted to a popular social media service. A complete architecture of a system that implements this idea is proposed and implemented, where Brain Pattern Analysis is performed using an Electroencephalogram device and a mobile computing device." The emotion detection concept is used in this book in Section 2.4.1, Electroencephalogram (EEG) Robustness in Patterns of Individual Differences and Similarities, to provide similar features that individuals share when detecting emotion and subsequently detecting intentions using similar features, including the P300 ERP.

4) On the Possibility of Insider Threat Detection Using Physiological Signal Processing [115]. Published in *Proceedings of the 7th International Conference on Security of Information and Networks'*14.

"Insider threat damages vary from intellectual property loss and fraud to IT sabotage. As insider threat incidents have evolved to cause potentially catastrophic damages, there exists a need for a detection mechanism in order to build solutions that prevent such threats. Studies over the years show an understanding of the threat, and many approaches have been suggested to detect it, yet none of the approaches targets the physiological aspect of the threat. Bio-signals are impossible to mimic or change, as opposed to behavioral approaches. In this paper, we investigate the use of physiological signals as a measurement to detect insider threat. We design an insider threat monitoring system called Physiological Signals Monitoring

(PSM) that detects incidents seconds before they occur. The main measurement in PSM is the abnormal deviation rate of electrocardiogram (ECG) amplitude, Galvanic Skin Response (GSR) and skin temperature that occurs seconds before an incident is executed. Our experiment on 15 human subjects explores this new area and shows the promise of the proposed solution with all of the tested incidents being correctly classified with Nearest Neighbor and Functional Trees classifiers." This paper was used in this book as a future improvement of IBAC in order to monitor insiders continuously, since IBAC is vulnerable if a malicious intention is developed after a user has been granted access.

5) On the Possibility of Insider Threat Prevention Using Intent-based Access Control (IBAC) [122]. Published in IEEE Systems Journal Special Issue in the Insider Threat, June 2015.

"Existing access control mechanisms are based on the concept of identity enrolment and recognition, and assume that recognized identity is a synonym to ethical actions, yet statistics over the years show that the most severe security breaches are the results of trusted, identified, and legitimate users who turned into malicious insiders. Insider threat damages vary from intellectual property loss and fraud to IT sabotage. As insider threat incidents evolve, there exist demands for a non-identity based authentication measure that rejects access to authorized individuals who have mal-intents of access. In this paper, we study the possibility of using the user's intention as an access control measure using the involuntary Electroencephalogram reactions towards visual stimuli. We propose Intent-based Access Control (IBAC) that detects the intentions of access based on the existence of knowledge about an intention. IBAC takes advantage of the robustness of Concealed Information Test (CIT) to assess access risk. We use the intent and intent motivation level to compute the access risk. Based on the calculated risk and risk accepted threshold, the system makes the decision whether to grant or deny access requests. We assessed the model using experiments on 30 participants that proved the robustness of the proposed solution." This journal article includes much of the work presented in this book and was published in the IEEE System Journal Special Issue in the Insider Threat.

Bibliography

[1] A. K. Jain, A. Ross, and S. Prabhakar, "An introduction to biometric recognition," IEEE Trans. Circuits Systems Video Technol. vol. 14, no. 1, pp. 4–20, 2004.

[2] G. Jackson, (2012). *Predicting Malicious Behavior: Tools and Techniques for Ensuring Global Security*. Hoboken, NJ: John Wiley & Sons, 2012.

[3] T. Armerding, "Why we can't stop malicious insiders," June 17, 2013. Available: http://www.csoonline.com/article/735047/why-we-can-t-stop-malicious-insiders-

[iv] A. Puusa and U. Tolvanen, "Organizational Identity and Trust," Available: http://ejbo.jyu.fi/pdf/ejbo_vol11_no2_pages_29-33.pdf

[5] The Globe and Mail. "Canadian spy Jeffery Delisle gets 20 years for selling secrets to Russia." February 8, 2013. Available: http://www.theglobeandmail.com/news/national/canadian-spy-jeffrey-delisle-gets-20-years-for-selling-secrets-to-russia/article8390425".

[6] D. M. Cappelli, A. P. Moore, and R. F. Trzeciak, *The CERT Guide to Insider Threats: How to Prevent, Detect, and*

Respond to Information Technology Crimes (1st ed.). Addison-Wesley Professional, 2012.

[7] "DoD Insider Threat Mitigation. Final Report of the Insider Threat Integrated Process Team." US Department of Defense, Office of the Assistant Secretary of Defense (Command, Control, Commuications, and Intelligence). Available: https://acc.dau.mil/CommunityBrowser.aspx?id=37478

[8] *Common Sense Guide to Mitigating Insider Threats*, 4th Edition, Dec. 2012. Available: http://www.sei.cmu.edu/library/abstracts/reports/12tr012.cfm

[9] "As cybercrime threats continue to escalate, 2013 State of Cybercrime Survey from PwC and CSO finds companies aren't doing enough to defend themselves," Available: http://www.pwc.com/us/en/increasing-it-effectiveness/publications/us-state-of-cybercrime.jhtml

[10] The CERT Insider Threat Center. Available: http://www.cert.org/insider_threat/

[11] S. Perreault and S. Brennan, 2010. "Criminal victimization in Canada," *Juristat*. vol. 30, no. 2. Statistics Canada Catalogue no. 85-002-X, 2009.

[12] Y. Song, M. Salem, S. Hershkop, and S. Stolfo, "System level user behavior biometrics using Fisher features and Gaussian mixture models," 2013 IEEE Security and Privacy Workshops.

[13] W. Young, H. Goldberg, A. Memory, J. Sartain, and T. Senator, "Use of domain knowledge to detect insider threats in computer Activities," IEEE Security and Privacy Workshops, 2013.

[14] D. Muchene, K. Luli, and C. Shue, "Reporting insider threats via covert channels," IEEE Security and Privacy Workshops, 2013.

[15] J. Hunker and C. Probst, "Insiders and Insider Threats: An Overview of Definitions and Mitigation Techniques," Available: http://isyou.info/jowua/papers/jowua-v2n1-1.pdf

[16] M. Guennoun, N. Abbad, J. Talom, S. M. M. Rahman, and K. El-Khatib, "Continuous Authentication by Electrocardiogram Data," IEEE TIC-STH 2009.

[17] D.F. Ferraiolo and D.R. Kuhn, "Role-Based Access Control," 15th National Computer Security Conference. pp. 554–563, Oct. 1992.

[18] "A Survey on Access Control Models," National Institution of Standards and Technology, Computer Security Division, Available: http://csrc.nist.gov/news_events/privilege-management-workshop/PvM-Model-Survey-Aug26-2009.pdf, Aug., 2009.

[19] D.F. Ferraiolo and D.R. Kuhn, "Role-Based Access Control," 15th National Computer Security Conference. pp. 554–563, Oct. 1992.

[20] G. Boella, & L. van der Torre, (2003). Access Control in Virtual Communities. In Proceedings of the IAT/WI 03 Workshop on Knowledge Grid and Grid Intelligence.

[21] J. Wang, Y. Takata, and H. Seki, " HBAC: A model for history-based access control and its model checking," Computer Security – ESORICS, 2006.

[22] J. Hur, and D. Noh, "Attribute-based access control with efficient revocation in data outsourcing systems," *Parallel and Distributed Systems*, 2011.

[23] G. Ma, K. Wu, T. Zhang, and W. Li, "A flexible policy-based access control model for Workflow Management Systems," *Computer Science and Automation Engineering* (CSAE), 2011.

[24] "Context-based access control," Available: http://www.cisco.com/c/en/us/support/ docs/security/ios-firewall/13814-32.html

[25] R. McGraw. "Risk-Adaptable Access Control (RAdAC)." National Institution of Standards and Technology, Computer Security Division, Available: http://csrc.nist.gov/news_events/privilege-management-workshop/radac-Paper0001.pdf

[26] R. Franziska, K. Tadayoshi, A. Moshchuk, B. Parno, H. Wang, "Providing Intent-Based Access To User-Owned Resources," U.S. Patent: 20130205385, Issued date August, 2013

[27] R. Kirsch and A. and Au, "EMG-based motion intention detection for control of a shoulder neuroprosbook," *Engineering in Medicine and Biology Society*, 1997.

[28] E. Lew, R. Chavarriaga, H. Zhang, M. Seeck, and J. Millan, "Self-paced movement intention detection from human brain signals: Invasive and non-invasive EEG," *Engineering in Medicine and Biology Society* (EMBC), 2012.

[29] M. Ishak, "Classification of EEG Signal for Movement Intentions-based Brain Computer Interfaces," International Journal of Advances in Computer Science and Technology (IJACST), Vol.3, No.11, Pages: 07-12 Dec. 2014

[30] Y. Nakauchi, K. Nogichi, P. Somwang, and T. Matsubara, "Human intention detection and activity support system for ubiquitous sensor room," *Intelligent Robots and Systems* (IROS 2003), 27-31 Oct. 2003.

[31] "nemesysco" Voice analysis technology, 2000. Available at: www.nemesysco.com. Accessed February 15, 2013.

[32] A. Elkins, J. Burgoon, and J. Nunamaker, "Vocal analysis software for security screening: Validity and deception detection potential," Homeland Security Affairs. Available: http://www.hsaj.org/?special:fullarticle=0.4.1.

[33] J. Burgoon, M. Adkins, J. Kruse, M. Jensen, T. Meservy, D. Twitchell, A. Deokar, and J. Nunamaker, "An approach for intent identification by building on deception detection,"

Proceedings of the 38th Annual Hawaii International Conference on System Sciences (HICSS '05), 2005.

[34] H. Chen, W. Chung, J. Qin, E. Reid, M. Sageman, and G. Weimann, "Uncovering the dark Web: A case study of Jihad on the Web," *Journal of the American Society for Information Science and Technology*, vol. 59, issue 8, Jun. 2008.

[35] T. Raghu and H. Chen, "Cyberinfrastructure for homeland security: Advances in information sharing, data mining, and collaboration systems,"*Decision Support Systems*, vol. 43, no. 4, pp. 1321-1323, 2007.

[36] N. Memon, J. Hu, D. Hicks, and H. Chen, *Social Network Data Mining: Research Questions, Techniques, and Applications, I: Data Mining for Social Network Data*. vol. 12. Editors J. Xu, D. Hicks, and H. Chen. Springer Publishing Company, 2010, pp. 1-7.

[37] N. Memon, H. Larsen, D. Hicks, and N. Harkiolakis, "Detecting hidden hierarchy in terrorist networks: Some case studies," *Intelligence and Security Informatics*, Springer, pp. 477-489, 2008.

[38] O. Vybornova, I. Smirnov, I. Sochenkov, A. Kiselyov, I. Tikhomirov, N. Chudova, Y. Kuznetsova, and G. Osipov, "Social tension detection and intention recognition using natural language semantic analysis: On the material of Russian-speaking social networks and Web forums,"

Intelligence and Security Informatics Conference (EISIC), 2011 European, Sept. 2011.

[39] N. Naveed, T. Gottron, J. Kunegis, and A. Alhadi, "Bad news travels fast: A Content-based analysis of interestingness on Twitter," Institute for Web Science and Technologies, University of Koblenz-Landau, 2011.

[40] Future Attribute Screening Technology (FAST) U.S. Homeland Security. Available: "www.dhs.gov/xlibrary/assets/privacy/privacy_pia_st_fast-a.pdf"

[41] "Homeland Security's 'Pre-Crime' Screening Will Never Work," *The Atlantic*, April 17, 2012, Available: http://www.theatlantic.com/technology/archive/2012/04/ homeland-securitys-pre-crime-screening-will-never-work/255971/

[42] S.Dong, S. Lee, "Understanding human implicit intention based on frontal electroencephalography (EEG)," in Neural Networks (IJCNN), The 2012 International Joint Conference on , vol., no., pp.1-5, 10-15 June 2012

[43] B.H. Sheppard, J. Hartwick, and P.R. Warshaw, "The theory of reasoned action: A meta-analysis of past research with recommendations for modifications and future research," *Journal of Consumer Research*, vol. 15, pp. 325–343, 1988.

[44] "necomimi" selected in "TIME Magazine / The 50 best inventions of the year," Retrieved on May 29, 2012, Available: Neurowear.com

[45] "intendiX-SOCI: g.tec Introduces Mind-controlled Computer Gaming at CeBIT2012". PR Newswire. March 5, 2012.

[46] K. Revett, and S.T. Magalhes, "Cognitive biometrics: Challenges for the future," *Global Security, Safety, and Sustainability*, vol. 92.. pp. 79–86, 2012.

[47] J. Thorpe, P.C. Van Oorschot, and A. Somayaji, "Pass-thoughts: Authenticating with our minds," In *Proceedings of the 2005 Workshop on New Security Paradigms* (NSPW '05) (New York, NY, USA), ACM pp. 45–56, 2005.

[48] M.K. Abdullah, K.S. Subari, J.L.C. Loong, and N.N.Ahmad, "Analysis of effective channel placement for an EEG-based biometric system," *2010 IEEE EMBS Conference on Biomedical Engineering and Sciences* (IECBES), pp. 303-306.

[49] A. Zúquete, B. Quintela, and J.P. Silva Chuna, "Biometric authentication using brain responses to visual stimuli," *Biosignals*, 2010.

[50] C. Miyamoto, S. Baba, and I. Nakanishi, "Biometric person authentication using new spectral features of electroencephalogram (EEG)," *Intelligent Signal Processing and Communications Systems*, 2008.

[51] S. Marcel and J. Millan, "Person authentication using brainwaves (EEG) and maximum a posteriori model adaptation." IEEE Transactions on Pattern Analysis and Machine Intelligence, vol. 29, no. 4, pp. 743-752, Apr. 2007.

[52] R. Palaniappan, "Two-stage biometric authentication method using thought activity brain waves," *International Journal of Neural Systems*, vol. 18, pp. 59-66, 2008.

[53] C. He, X. Lv, and Z.J. Wang, "Hashing the mAR coefficients from EEG data for person authentication," *IEEE International Conference on Acoustics, Speech and Signal Processing* (ICASSP 2009),2009.

[54] I. Svogor and T. Kisasondi, "Two factor authentication using EEG augmented passwords", Proceedings of the ITI 2012 34th International Conference on Information Technology Interfaces (ITI) 2012.

[55] I. Nakanishi, S. Baba, and C. Miyamoto, "EEG based biometric authentication using new spectral features," *International Symposium on Intelligent Signal Processing and Communication Systems*, pp. 651-654, 2009.

[56] V. Balakrishnan and P.H.P. Yeow, "A study of the effect of thumb sizes on mobile phone texting satisfaction," *Journal of Usability Studies*, vol. 3, issue 3, pp. 118-128, May 2008.

[57] V. Balakrishnan and P.H.P. Yeow, "Hand-Size variations effect on mobile phone texting satisfaction," *Ubiquitous*

Computing and Communication Journal, vol. 2, no. 5, pp. 115-122, 2007.

[58] C. Conati, "Probabilistic assessment of user's emotions in educational games," *Applied Artificial Intelligence*, vol. 16, no. 7-8, pp. 555-575, Aug. 2002.

[59] D. Matsumoto and H.S. Hwang, "Reading facial expressions of emotion," *Psychological Science Agenda*, American Psychological Association, May 2011.

[60] M. Fabiani, D. Karis, and E. Donchin, "P300 and recall in an incidental memory paradigm,".*Psychophysiology*, vol. 23, pp. 298-308, 1986.

[61] A. Magliero, T.R. Bashore, M.G.H. Coles, and E. Donchin, "On the dependence of P300 latency on stimulus evaluation processes," Psychophysiology, vol. 21, pp. 171-186,1984.

[62] R. Mertens and J. Polich, "P300 from a single-stimulus paradigm: Passive versus active tasks and stimulus modality," *Electroencephalogr Clin.* vol. 104, pp. 488-497, 1997a.

[63] J. Polich, "On the relationship between EEG and P300: Individual differences, aging, and ultradian rhythms," *Int J Psychophysiol*, vol. 26, pp. 299-317, 1997.

[64] H. Ekanayake, "P300 and Emotiv EPOC: Does Emotiv EPOC capture real EEG?" Research use of Emotiv EPOC, Available: http://neurofeedback.visaduma.info/P300nEmotiv.pdf, Dec. 2010.

[65] F.H. Duffy and H. Als, "A stable pattern of EEG spectral coherence distinguishes children with autism from neuro-typical controls - A large case control study," *BMC Med,* vol. 10, p. 64, 2012.

[66] D.J. Krusienski, E.W. Sellers, F. Cabestaing, S. Bayoudh, D.J. Mcfarland, T.M. Vaughan, and J.R. Wolpaw, "A comparison of classification techniques for the P300 Speller," *Journal of Neural Engineering,* vol. 3, issue 4, pp. 299-305, Dec. 2006.

[67] B. Blankertz, "Bci competitions webpage," [Online]. Available: http://www.bbci.de/competition/

[68] A. Rakotomamonjy, and V. Guigue, "BCI Competition III: Dataset II - Ensemble of SVMs for BCI P300 Speller," *IEEE Transactions on Biomedical Engineering,* Mar. 2008.

[69] M. Kaper, P. Meinicke, U. Grossekathoefer, T. Lingner, and [add initial].Ritter, "BCI competition 2003 -data set IIb: support vector machines for the P300 speller paradigm," *IEEE Transactions on Biomedical Engineering,* vol. 51, no. 6, 2004.

[70] S. Costagliola, B. Dal Seno, and M. Mateucchi, "Recognition and classification of P300s in EEG signals by means of feature extraction using wavelet decomposition," *Proceeding of International Joint Conference on Neural Networks,* 2009.

[71] D. Krapohl, J. McCloughan, and S. Senter. "How to use the Concealed Information Test," *Polygraph,* 2009.

[72] D. Carmel, E. Dayan, A. Naveh, O. Raveh, and G. Ben-Shakhar, :Estimating the validity of the guilty knowledge test from simulated experiments: The external validity of mock crime studies," *Journal of Experimental Psychology: Applied*, vol. 9, pp. 261-269, 2003.

[73] G. Ben-Shakhar and E. Elaad, "The validity of psychophysiological detection of information with the guilty knowledge test: A meta-analytic review," *Journal of Applied Psychology*, vol. 88, no. 1, pp. 131-151, 2003.

[74] Harrington v. State, Case No. PCCV 073247. Iowa District Court for Pottawattamie County, March 5, 2001.

[75] L.A. Farwell, "Brain fingerprinting: A comprehensive tutorial review of detection of concealed information with event-related brain potentials", 2012, DOI 10.1007/s11571-012-9192-2, *Cognitive Neurodynamics*, vol. 6, pp. 115–54. Accessed May 1, 2013.

[76] L.A. Farwell and T. Makeig, "Farwell Brain Fingerprinting in the case of Harrington v. State." Open Court X,3:7-10, Indiana State Bar Assoc. Available at: Farwell and Makeig on Brain Fingerprinting in ''Harrington v. State'' in ''Open Court'', 2005.

[77] Science Daily, "Brain scans might predict future criminal behavior," Available: http://www.sciencedaily.com/releases/2013/03/130328125319.htm. May 2013.

[78] J. Rosenfeld, X. Hu, E. Labkovsky, E. Meixner, and M. Winograd, "Review of recent studies and issues regarding the P300-based complex trial protocol for detection of concealed information," *International Journal of Psychophysiology*, Nov. 2013.

[79] J. Meixner and P. Rosenfeld, "A mock terrorism application of the P300-based concealed information test," Society for Psychology Research, Wiley 2010.

[80] S. Perreault and S. Brennan, "Criminal victimization in Canada, 2009." Juristat. vol. 30, no. 2. Statistics Canada Catalogue no. 85-002-X, 2010.

[81] B.J. Fogg, "A behavior model for persuasive design," In *Proceedings of the 4th International Conference on Persuasive Technology* (Persuasive '09). ACM, New York, NY, USA, Article 40, 7 pages. DOI=10.1145/1541948.1541999 http://doi.acm.org/10.1145/1541948.1541999, 2009.

[82] M.K. Abdullah, K.S. Subari, J.L.C. Loong, and N.N. Ahmad, "Analysis of effective channel placement for an EEG-based biometric system," *2010 IEEE EMBS Conference on Biomedical Engineering and Sciences* (IECBES), pp. 303-306, 2010.

[83] A. Zúquete, B. Quintela, and J.P. Silva Chuna, "Biometric authentication using brain responses to visual stimuli," *Biosignals* 2010.

[84] C. Miyamoto, S. Baba, and I. Nakanishi, "Biometric person authentication using new spectral features of electroencephalogram (EEG)," *Intelligent Signal Processing and Communications Systems* (ISPACS), 2008.

[85] S. Kleih, S. Halder, F. Nijboer, and A. Kübler, "Motivation modulates the P300 Amplitude during BCI use," International Federation of Clinical Neurophysiology, 2010.

[86] R. Holton, "Intention and weakness of will," Journal of Philosophy, vol. 96, pp. 241-62, 1999.

[87] Dobson, Michael S., and Deborah S. Dobson. "Chapter 4 - Tools for Qualitative Risk Analysis". Project Risk and Cost Analysis. AMACOM. © 2012. Books24x7.

[88] Goodpasture, John. "Chapter 8 - Special Topics in Quantitative Management". Quantitative Methods in Project Management. J. Ross Publishing. © 2004. Books24x7.

[89] Office of Government Commerce (OGC), The. "Appendix B - Common Techniques". Management of Risk: Guidance for Practitioners. TSO, Ltd. © 2010. Books24x7

[90] S.J. Luck, "Ten Simple Rules for Designing and Interpreting ERP Experiments," In Handy, T. C., (ED.), *Event-Related Potentials: A Method Handbook*. Cambridge MA: MIT Press.

[91] Emotiv EPOC "http://emotiv.wikia.com/wiki/Emotiv_EPOC" Accessed in April, 2013.

[92] P.G. Fitzgerald and T.W. Picton, "The effects of probability and discriminability on the evoked potentials to unpredictable stimuli," *Ann N Y Acad Sci.* vol. 425, pp. 199-203, 1984.

[93] C.J. Gonsalvez and J. Polich, "P300 amplitude is determined by target-to-target interval," *Psychophysiology*, vol. 39, no. 3, pp. 388-396, 2002.

[94] HyperCam, Available: http://hypercam.en.softonic.com/

[95] EEGLAB - Open Source Matlab Toolbox for Electrophysiological Research.Available; http://sccn.ucsd.edu/eeglab/

[96] EEGLAB, "Chapter 04: Preprocessing Tools," Available: http://sccn.ucsd.edu/wiki/Chapter_04:_Preprocessing_Tools

[97] M. Hall, E. Frank, G. Holmes, B. Pfahringer, P. Reutemann, and I. Witten, "The WEKA Data Mining Software: An Update," *SIGKDD Explorations*, vol. 11, issue 1, 2009.

[98] ERPLAB - Open source MATLAB toolbox for ERP analysis," Available: http://www.erpinfo.org/

[99] Straight Healthcare, "Sensitivity vs specificity," Available: http://www.straighthealthcare.com/sensitivity-specificity-figure.html. Accessed September 21, 2014.

[100] R. Bolle, J. Connell, S. Pankanti, N. Ratha, and A. Senior, "Guide to Biometrics," ISBN: 0-387-40089-3, New York: Springer, 2003.

[101] PBS Innovation Series – "Brain Fingerprinting," May 4, 2004. "Brain Fingerprinting: Ask the Experts," Accessed May 1, 2013.

[102] J.P. Rosenfeld, "Brain fingerprinting: A critical analysis," The Scientific Review of Mental Health Practice, vol. 4, no. 1 (Spring/Summer 2005) pp. 20-37, Available: http://groups.psych.northwestern.edu/rosenfeld/NewFiles/BF critiquerevsub3-6.pdf, last visited May 01, 2013.

[103] "Information Technology Standards," Available at: www.iso27001security.com

[104] Hao-Yu Wu, Michael Rubinstein, Eugene Shih, John Guttag, Frédo Durand, William T. Freeman "Eulerian Video Magnification for Revealing Subtle Changes in the World" ACM Transactions on Graphics, Volume 31, Number 4 (Proc. SIGGRAPH), 2012

[105] MailOnline, "The hi-tech tattoo that could replace ALL your passwords: Motorola reveals plans for ink and even pills to identify us," Available: http://www.dailymail.co.uk/ sciencetech/article-2333203/Moto-X-Motorola-reveals-plans- ink-pills-replace-ALL-passwords.html

[106] Emotiv Insight, Available: http://emotivinsight.com

[107] Privacy by Design Resolution. Jerusalem: 32nd International Conference of Data Protection and Privacy Commissioners (2010). Available: http://www.ipc.on.ca

/site_documents/pbd-resolution.pdf

[108] R. Cappelli, A. Lumini, D. Maio, and D. Maltoni, "Fingerprint Image Reconstruction from Standard Templates," *IEEE Transactions*, vol. 29, pp. 1489-1503, 2007.

[109] P. Mohanty, S. Sarkar, and R. Kasturi, "Privacy and security issues related to match cores," in *IEEE Workshop on Privacy Research in Vision*, CVPRW, 2006.

[110] S.J. Luck, "Design of ERP experiments," ERP Boot Camp, 2013. Available: http://erpinfo.org/boot-camp-2007-materials/2013-boot-camp-materials/lecture-notes/08-%20Design%20of%20ERP%20Experiments.pdf

[111] J. Rosenfeld, E. Labkovsky, M. Winograd, M. Lui, C. Vandenboom, and E. Chedid, "The Complex Trial Protocol (CTP): A new, countermeasure-resistant, accurate, P300-based method for detection of concealed information," *Psychophysiology*, vol. 45, pp. 906-919, 2008.

[112] J.P. Rosenfeld, E. Labkovsky, M. Winograd, M.A. Lui, C. Vandenboom, and E. Chedid, "The Complex Trial Protocol (CTP): A new, countermeasure-resistant, accurate, P300-based method for detection of concealed information," *Psychophysiology*, vol. 45, pp. 906-919, 2008.

[113] A. Rao, M. Georgeff, "BDI agents: From Theory to Practice," Proceedings of the First International Conference on Multiagent Systems, 1995.

[114] J. Rushby, "Design and Verification of Secure Systems". 8th ACM Symposium on Operating System Principles. Pacific Grove, California, US. pp. 12–21, 1981

[115] A. Almehmadi and K. El-Khatib, "On the possibility of insider threat detection using physiological signal monitoring," *In Proceedings of the 7th International Conference on Security of Information and Networks* (SIN '14), ACM, New York, NY, USA, pp. 223-230, 2014.

[116] NeXus-10 MKII, Available: http://www.mindmedia.nl/CMS/en/products/nexus-systems/item/175-nexus10mkii.html

[117] A. Almehmadi and K. El-Khatib, "Authorized! Access denied, Unauthorized! Access granted," *In Proceedings of the 6th International Conference on Security of Information and Networks* (SIN '13), 2013.

[118] CNN, "A grisly tale: Fetus cut from womb when woman answers Craigslist ad," March 20, 2015, Available: http://www.cnn.com/2015/03/19/us/craigslist-pregnant-woman-womb-baby-removed/

[119] Daily News, "Body of missing CSUN student Abdullah Alkadi found in Palm Desert," October 17, 2014, Available: http://www.dailynews.com/general-news/20141017/body-of-missing-csun-student-abdullah-alkadi-found-in-palm-desert.

[120] A. Almehmadi, and K. El-Khatib, "The state of the art in electroencephalogram and access control," *In Proceedings of*

the Third International Conference on Communications and Information Technology (ICCIT), 2013, pp.49-54, 2013 doi: 10.1109/ICCITechnology.2013.6579521

[121] A. Almehmadi, M. Bourque, K. El-Khatib, "A Tweet of the Mind: Automated Emotion Detection for Social Media Using Brain Wave Pattern Analysis," *In Proceedings of the International Conference on Social Computing* (SocialCom), 2013, vol., no., pp.987-991

[122] A. Almehmadi, and K. El-Khatib, "On the Possibility of Insider Threat Prevention Using Intent-Based Access Control (IBAC)," *IEEE Systems Journal*, vol., no.99, pp.1-12, May 2015